O9-BSA-040

LITERARY SELVES

Recent Titles in
Contributions to the Study of World Literature

Comic Tales of the Middle Ages: An Anthology and Commentary
Marc Wolterbeek

Framing the *Canterbury Tales*: Chaucer and the Medieval Frame Narrative Tradition
Katharine S. Gittes

There Is No Truer Truth: The Musical Aspect of Browning's Poetry
Nachum Schoffman

Reworlding: The Literature of the Indian Diaspora
Emmanuel S. Nelson, editor

Caliban in Exile: The Outsider in Caribbean Fiction
Margaret Paul Joseph

Sitting at the Feet of the Past: Retelling the North American Folktale for Children
Gary D. Schmidt and Donald R. Hettinga, editors

The Anna Book: Searching for Anna in Literary History
Mickey Pearlman, editor

Writing and Reality: A Study of Modern British Diary Fiction
Andrew Hassam

Shakespeare's Proverbial Themes: A Rhetorical Context for the Sententia as *Res*
Marjorie Donker

Promptings of Desire: Creativity and the Religious Impulse in the Works of D. H. Lawrence
Paul Poplawski

The Second Best Bed: Shakespeare's Will in a New Light
Joyce E. Rogers

LITERARY SELVES

Autobiography and Contemporary American Nonfiction

James N. Stull

CONTRIBUTIONS TO THE STUDY OF WORLD LITERATURE, NUMBER 50

Greenwood Press
Westport, Connecticut • London

Library of Congress Cataloging-in-Publication Data

Stull, James N.
Literary selves : autobiography and contemporary American nonfiction / James N. Stull.
p. cm.—(Contributions to the study of world literature, ISSN 0738–9345 ; no. 50)
Includes bibliographical references and index.
ISBN 0–313–28825–9 (alk. paper)
1. American prose literature—20th century—History and criticism. 2. Authors, American—Biography—History and criticism. 3. Self in literature. 4. Autobiography. I. Title. II. Series.
PS366.A88S85 1993
818′.50809—dc20 93–10376

British Library Cataloguing in Publication Data is available.

Library of Congress Catalog Card Number: 93–10376
ISBN: 0–313–28825–9
ISSN: 0738–9345

First published in 1993

Greenwood Press, 88 Post Road West, Westport, CT 06881
An imprint of Greenwood Publishing Group, Inc.

Printed in the United States of America

The paper used in this book complies with the Permanent Paper Standard issued by the National Information Standards Organization (Z39.48–1984).

10 9 8 7 6 5 4 3 2

Copyright Acknowledgments

The author and publisher are grateful to the following sources for permission to reprint material:

An earlier version of chapter 2 appeared as James N. Stull, "Self and the Performance of Others: The Pastoral Vision of John McPhee," *North Dakota Quarterly* 59, no. 3 (Summer 1991): 182–200.

Portions of chapter 4 appeared in James N. Stull, "The Cultural Gamesmanship of Tom Wolfe," *Journal of American Culture* 14, no. 3 (Fall 1991): 25–30.

Portions of chapter 5 appeared in James N. Stull, "Telling Stories About Miami," *The Canadian Review of American Studies* 20, no. 2 (Fall 1989): 265–270. Used by permission of the University of Calgary.

An earlier version of chapter 6 appeared as James N. Stull, "Hunter S. Thompson: A Ritual Reenactment of Deviant Behavior," *Connecticut Review* XIII, no. 1 (Spring 1991): 87–99. Used by permission of the Board of Trustees of the Connecticut State University.

Excerpts from *Slouching Towards Bethlehem* by Joan Didion. Copyright ©1968 by Joan Didion. Reprinted by permission of Farrar, Straus and Giroux, Inc.; also used by permission of Andre Deutsch Ltd.

Excerpts from *The White Album* by Joan Didion. Copyright ©1979 by Joan Didion. Reprinted by permission of Farrar, Straus and Giroux, Inc.; also used by permission of Weidenfeld and Nicolson.

Excerpts from *The Armies of the Night* by Norman Mailer. Copyright ©1968 by Norman Mailer. Used by permission of New American Library, a division of Penguin Books USA Inc.; also used by permission of the author and his agents, Scott Meredith Literary Agency, Inc., 845 Third Avenue, New York, NY 10022.

Contents

Acknowledgments

Work on this book began several years ago. Over this period of time, a number of people were helpful and supportive. I would like to take this opportunity to thank them. First, a special thanks goes to William M. Murray and Albert E. Stone, both of whom read the manuscript more than once and always offered judicious suggestions and criticism. I would also like to thank Richard P. Horwitz, Dennis M. Moore, Nancy K. Barry, and Barry H. Leeds. All of these people read the manuscript in part or as a whole and also made valuable suggestions. Most of all, I want to thank Elaine, who provided continued support through the entire writing process.

1

Introduction: Presentations of Self in Contemporary American Literary Nonfiction

In "The Self as History: Reflections on Autobiography," Alfred Kazin explains that "the deepest side of being an American is the sense of being like nothing before us in history."[1] This culturally shared belief is central to understanding our country's foundation myth, and it is also implicitly reaffirmed in a socio-economic system that aggrandizes the self and nominally celebrates not only the lives of the rich, well-known, and famous but ordinary people as well. While writing about the self, as Georges Gusdorf points out, "expresses a concern peculiar to Western man, a concern that has been of good use in his systematic conquest of the universe,"[2] it is also a mode of expression that seems ideally and more specifically suited to the optimism of the American spirit, to our faith in the value of individual action in a democratic and pluralistic society. Autobiographical writing—to tell one's own story—has provided an avenue for many Americans to declare their "individual difference against the assumptions of a larger and determining national destiny."[3]

The Autobiography of Benjamin Franklin, *Walden*, *The Education of Henry Adams*, the *Narrative of the Life of Frederick Douglass*, *Let Us Now Praise Famous Men*, and *Black Boy* all testify to both the variety and enduring importance of personal history and autobiographical writing in our literary and cultural heritage. Since World War II, nonfiction prose has become even more central to American life; various modes of autobiographical writing—testament, confession, journal and diary, memoir, and personal journalism—have flourished during the post-war years. James Cox points out that autobiographical writing becomes more germane "when history and politics seem to possess the very drama we seek for in stage and fictive experience in periods of equanimity and peace."[4] Francis Russell Hart more pointedly notes that specific modes of autobiographical writing are more (or less) relevant in different periods of American life: "confession abounds in a time of soul-searching," for example, and "apology in times of confrontation."[5] As these comments suggest, pivotal junctures in our social and political life are indirectly reflected or embodied in conflicts of identity in the American citizenry. This is perhaps most evident in the numerous ethnic, black, and feminist autobiographies published in the last thirty years. *The Autobiography of Malcolm X*, *I Know Why the Caged Bird Sings* (Maya Angelou), *Soledad Brother* (George Jackson), *The Woman Warrior* (Maxine Hong Kingston), *Zami: A New Spelling of My Name* (Audre Lorde), *Bronx Primitive* (Kate Simon), and many other autobiographical works challenge cultural and sexual stereotypes and ethnocentric conceptions of identity by identifying the self as the locus and barometer of social and political change. These texts comprise, of course, only a small portion of a wide range of autobiographical writings that subtly reflect the diversity of contemporary American experience. This work, *Literary Selves: Autobiography and Contemporary American Nonfiction*, represents an effort to characterize and discuss another small segment of this recent phenomenon by focusing on the complex relations between the singular self and its world as it is articulated in the collected and very different works of six contemporary American literary journalists: John McPhee, Joe McGinniss, Tom Wolfe, Joan Didion, Hunter S. Thompson, and Norman Mailer.

Since the early 1970s, literary and cultural critics have proposed a variety of theories and critical positions in an attempt to affirm the generic status of literary nonfiction, often identified as the New Journalism, and codify the means by which academicians might make sense of it. More often than not, they interpreted this varied collection of writings in literary terms, usually "realist" or "postmodernist," and focused on a limited number of canonical works: Truman Capote's *In Cold Blood*, Norman Mailer's *The Armies of the Night*, and Tom Wolfe's *The Electric Kool-Aid Acid Test*. As Chris Anderson points out, critics have principally been concerned "with the larger question of genre, with the relationship between fiction and nonfiction, literature and journalism."[6] Numerous reviewers and critics have acknowledged the subjective and often highly personal nature of this writing. In fact, their "concentration on literary technique" has transformed "the history of the New Journalism into a triumph of individual sensibility."[7] Yet, they have largely ignored a critical and perhaps obvious dimension of nonfiction writing: the manner and ways literary journalists articulate a self, or selves, within their nonfiction texts and metaphorical worlds.

While it is not my intention to propose a highly elaborate methodological framework, I would like to briefly discuss—before I turn to the texts themselves—some of the various ways this group of literary journalists reveals and defines themselves in their discussions of contemporary American life. First and foremost, the testament of (an authorial) self is frequently discernible as the shaping presence behind the nonfiction text. In some instances, this is subtly revealed in the structure of the narrative. The highly fragmented and self-reflexive quest narratives of Hunter S. Thompson, for example, are compatible with his provisional understanding of identity and his articulation of an unstable and changing American society. The presence of the author is also revealed, however, in the very words themselves. As Chris Anderson explains in *Style As Argument: Contemporary American Nonfiction*, "the language of contemporary American nonfiction is not transparent but translucent. We are never able to look completely past the words on the page to the people and events they evoke; We are always aware of the words themselves."[8] Style is also an epistemological strategy that both reveals and defines reality, a "reality," I should emphasize, that is often a highly personal and metaphorical interpretation of material and social worlds. While contemporary nonfiction is indeed an "experience of style," it is also a testament of authorial selfhood and a means of verbal empowerment, a way of creating a self and arresting experience in the moment of language by symbolically possessing the world in the author's own distinct words. Autobiographical writing, Albert E. Stone maintains, "necessarily manifests by every word, image, episode, and chapter division the architectural presence and imaginative identity of its author. Style is indeed a self, if not the only self."[9]

Writers of creative nonfiction also identify the personal and ideological dimensions of their cultural and literary enterprises by writing, at times, in the first person and privileging the epistemological authority of the imperial self over the institutional procedures of conventional journalism: the "neutral" perspective of objectivity, dependence on official (and impersonal) sources, the grounding of "truth" in journalistic fact, and the use of the "inverted pyramid," which assures reader and journalist alike that facts can be chosen and arranged in a specific—and unquestioned—order of importance. The ascendance of the New Journalism in the 1960s was in part a response to and rejection of traditional journalistic objectivity, which Michael Schudson aptly describes as "an ideology of the distrust of the self."[10] The repudiation of traditional journalism forms and procedures means, of course, that some writers of creative nonfiction, past and present, not only privilege a participatory and/or observing self but also redefine their relationship to subject matter in often idiosyncratic or at least personal ways. Each literary journalist establishes a relative position to the event and assumes the journalistic role of either detached observer or involved participant, or some position in between. The role not only influences what literary journalists reveal about themselves but also determines the manner in which information is disclosed and how the reader is constructed and addressed.

In some instances, a literary journalist like John McPhee or George Plimpton defines the arena or setting where the event takes place. In other social contexts, the literary journalist—most notably a Norman Mailer or a Hunter S. Thompson—appropriates public occasions and transforms them into symbolic stages on which a "performing" self is enacted for readers who anticipate, even expect, such flamboyant and opportunistic behavior. As these examples suggest, the presentation of a literary and social self is routinely characterized by a self-consciousness unprecedented in more conventional works of journalism and nonfiction. In fact, a number of literary journalists are acutely aware that they are social role players and performers, donning provisional masks and participating in and later writing about events that often have a wide cultural appeal. In a number of the works I will discuss, the presentation of what I call the "performing self" represented a culturally acceptable way to present the self in a society—the 1960s and early 1970s—characterized increasingly by self-promotion and displays of exhibitionism, whether fornicating on stage during an off-Broadway play, wearing see-through blouses or miniskirts, or participating in a demonstration that could later be watched on the six o'clock news. While it might indeed be an overstatement to suggest that personal concepts of identity and presentations of self are based directly on models provided by society, Christopher Lasch points out that several historical trends "converged in our time to produce not merely in artists but in ordinary men and women an escalating cycle of self-consciousness—a sense of the self as a performer under the constant scrutiny of friends and strangers."[11] While this phenomenon was indeed evident in displays of "guerrilla" or "street" theater, presentations of Julian Beck's Living Theater, and other significant cultural moments, it is also central to understanding much of the literary journalism authored during this period in American life. The self-consciousness Lasch identifies in our social life is also reflected and affirmed in some contemporary works of nonfiction, most notably in the writings of Mailer, Didion, and Thompson. The lives (and personal moments) documented in their autobiographical works are often, as we shall see, the "lives lived in anticipation of that fact, lived in consciousness of their own narratability"[12] and in recognition, I would add, of their unique performance value.

While John McPhee, Joe McGinniss, Tom Wolfe, Joan Didion, Hunter S. Thompson, and Norman Mailer define relationships to society in terms uniquely their own—as a personal metaphor of self—the way in which they present a self, or selves, is understood and shared with many others in the culture. These often highly autobiographical works of creative nonfiction exist, moreover, within social, class, and journalistic communities and are the product of particular systems (ideologies) of thought. All of these writers define a self—reveal who they are—in relation to their subjects and metaphorical others. The identification the author/narrator/journalist experiences with subjects and readers can be relatively isomorphic or, as it frequently is in the works of Thompson and Mailer, one of complete opposition. The coherence of these textual and metaphorical worlds is based in part on the stability and uniformity of the author's self-concept, the unity (or lack of unity) attributed to the social and material worlds, and how closely, as I noted, the journalist defines a relation to others within the aforementioned communities. In other words, the degree to which the journalist identifies with his subjects constitutes a form of self-disclosure while it identifies a community of unified or disparate others. In effect, each work of literary journalism is either a ritual affirmation of community and/or a symbolic challenge to the social order. Irving Louis Horowitz explains that autobiographical writing not only gives shape and coherence to individual lives; it is a "social injunction"—a "rationalization, justification, and exhortation of the social vision."[13]

At times, this "social vision" or symbolic community is influenced by and based on displays of gender. Norman Mailer, Hunter S. Thompson, and other literary journalists, for example, often participate in and/or write about ritual male activities, playing professional sports (George Plimpton), traveling with the Hell's Angels (Thompson), or covering the Vietnam War (Michael Herr). In each instance, the author affirms a generic male identity by testing—at the risk of injury—his courage and physical prowess in confrontational moments. While this pattern of behavior is evident in numerous examples of literary journalism, other male writers of creative nonfiction assume a more detached, even "objective" role. This reveals, I believe, as much about the inability of some men to express emotions and establish relationships (with their subjects) as it does about their alleged commitment to the canons of objectivity and other journalistic conventions.

In addition to presenting a self in a way that has meaning within a broader social community, the literary journalist demonstrates how the self is, to some degree, uniquely different from anybody else. In part, a self is articulated and given shape when literary journalists offer revealing information about their private or personal lives. While this material may appear to be unnecessarily gratuitous, providing voyeuristic glimpses into the lives of celebrated and well-known writers, it is often critically important in establishing the perspective, or epistemological frame, through which the social world is chronicled and understood. A truthful journalism account requires, in other words, information about both the perceiving self and the objects (events) being perceived.

Moreover, the public declaration of personal and even private information can be meaningfully interpreted as a psychological expression of hidden identity. While it is difficult to extrapolate from bits of personal information, presentations of self can indeed be understood in psychological as well as social and ideological terms. "Behind historic identity," Albert E. Stone points out, "lurks another 'self' whose psychic structures and states reveal themselves symbolically through language. In fact, autobiography's coded imagery often speaks more truly than more literal renditions of experience, for it suggests patterns of deep continuity within personality."[14] These structures and patterns are embodied in the author's personal and often idiosyncratic statement of identity. The complex, fully rounded, psychological, social, and somatic self is crystalized into a more generalized and encompassing statement of self-identification—a metaphor of self—that defines literary journalists' relations to the world and reveals the essence of who they believe themselves to be. The autobiographical dimension of a work, in other words, is revealed in what Barbara Lounsberry calls "the personal 'mythos' of the writer—the degree to which the writer's own experience and traits, values, and ideals influence interaction with the nonfictional subject and determine a work's ultimate vision."[15] The underlying themes, rhetorical strategies, and methods of self-presentation all make up a rhetorical and metaphorical world that points to a material reality while simultaneously embodying the distinctive way in which the author understands a self and its world. The metaphor of self is not merely a literary persona, however; it is a statement about how the individual sees and interacts with and understands the world, about how the author embroiders a "coherent, richly meaningful, intensely organized, altogether self-oriented universe."[16] James Olney maintains that metaphors reveal "very little about what the world is, or is like, but a great deal about what I am, or am like, and about what I am becoming."[17] While a metaphor of self might be a cumulation or product of past experiences, it provides a frame for understanding present and future experiences and, by connecting the "known of ourselves to the unknown of the world," it "organizes the self into a new and richer entity."[18]

The task of reconciling this personal statement of self with public expectations is often an implicit goal in many of these autobiographical efforts. Autobiographical writing dramatizes the complex relation—and tension—between individuals and their society; the "sovereign self" is presented, in other words, in relation to "a unique national selfhood, a heterogeneity within shared American ideals and aspirations."[19] As I hope to illustrate, these personal statements of identity might "be viewed as a collection" of certain "acts of self performance unified by shared cultural values and fashionable metaphors of self."[20] My intention, however, is not to make overarching generalizations based on a handful of canonical works. While focusing on the presentation of self—and making comparisons between writers and connections to the world outside the text—I am committed to a holistic appraisal of the collected works of a group of literary journalists who began writing nonfiction in the 1960s.

In chapter 2, I discuss how John McPhee conceptualizes an ideal and authentic imperial self that has its roots in the American past. More specifically, McPhee's conception of self is revealed through his discussion of a community of chosen subjects whose traditional values and beliefs are shared by the author and other members of society. In establishing the parameters of his journalistic contract, McPhee defines his subjects, perhaps incidentally so, as social and "heroic" performers. His methodological (journalistic) stance—as a detached, objective, and self-effacing observer—generally dictates that he reveal himself chiefly in the activities of watching and measuring the performances of others. His conception of an idealized and imperial self is in part predicated on the concentrated attention he devotes to his individual subjects. In certain works and specific textual moments McPhee is, of course, an involved participant as well as objective witness. What is critically important in most all of McPhee's writing, however, is that a relatively stable and uniform image of self and its world is affirmed in his implicit identification with the subjects who populate his metaphorical world. McPhee's construction of a stable, authentic, and old-fashioned American self is at once a retreat into certain pasts and a reaction to a social order increasingly characterized by fragmentation, the erosion of traditional values and beliefs, and the diminution of what was once called the imperial self.

In the nonfiction world of Joe McGinniss, we see a similar concern with the role individuals play in a changing American society. Like McPhee, McGinniss reveals an intense interest in the possibilities (and limitations) of a contemporary heroic self. While McPhee readily identifies traits that tend to idealize social others, McGinniss seems intent, perhaps unconsciously so, on exposing the flaws of his allegedly "heroic" and model subjects. The problems McGinniss identifies in the lives of his subjects reveal and reflect, most notably in *Heroes*, the spiritual crisis of the author as well as the troubles of a changing American society. This is most vividly and generally illustrated in his preoccupation with authority and the fall of symbolic and real father figures. This is a principal concern in at least four of McGinniss' works: *The Selling of the President 1968*, *Heroes*, *Fatal Vision*, and *Blind Faith*. If McPhee celebrates the promise of the American experience in his idealization of model American citizens, McGinniss implicitly—and often quite explicitly—suggests that our country's best days are behind us.

While John McPhee and Joe McGinniss assume the roles of participant journalist and detached observer, Tom Wolfe almost uniformly assumes the posture of a detached, erudite cultural critic. Whenever he does appear as a journalist (character) in his work—in *The Electric Kool-Aid Acid Test*, for example—he underscores his outsider status and assumes a role comparable to an ethnographer examining a foreign society or culture. Yet, what he finds significant in the lives of others—the symbolic detail of their status life—reflects how Wolfe presents himself to the world and reveals his understanding of personal and social identity. If McPhee articulates an inner-directed imperial self, Wolfe exhorts that the true self is largely determined by extrinsic factors, status details and status-group membership. While Wolfe cannot be considered a social performer in the sense that Norman Mailer and Hunter S. Thompson are, he assumes, however, the role of cultural critic cum literary fop. Moreover, while his journalistic deportment may indeed be more reserved than many of his contemporaries, his architectural and flamboyant presence is felt, as Chris Anderson and other critics have noted, in his dazzling prose style.

Unlike McPhee and Wolfe, Joan Didion constructs a more confessional and private self while acknowledging the conceptualization of a decidedly provisional identity (or identities) as the only possibility in postmodern society. Perhaps more than most other literary journalists, her writings are characterized by a detailed examination of intimate and private concerns. In *Slouching Towards Bethlehem*, for example, Didion enters her past and identifies the importance of a former, childhood self. She implicitly suggests that rapid historical change and social fragmentation make such personal and autobiographical recoveries essential. In *The White Album* Didion explores private preoccupations and fears in her very personal reading of a changing social world. At times, Didion hides a personal self behind the detached and nominally objective mask of the social critic. In both her personal essays and cultural criticism, however, we see a distinct reading of contemporary American experience that unifies and gives continuity to all her writings.

Hunter S. Thompson vividly dramatizes his adversarial relationship with an oppressive American society by constructing a real and metaphorical self as an outlaw and social deviant. While this persistent metaphor of self gives coherence to his distinctive experience and writing style, the ideal of a central, coherent identity, as it is articulated in the works of McPhee, entirely disappears. As Thompson chronicles his serendipitous adventures, he makes us increasingly aware that the social self is shaped by the manic and demonic realities of an eroding social structure. Like Norman Mailer, Thompson presents the journalistic self in an array of provisional masks, masks that take their chameleon-coloration from the circumstances and imperatives of the moment. Thompson repeatedly reminds the reader, furthermore, that writing is an artifice and a verbal construct. While he questions the validity of his journalistic enterprise, he nonetheless suggests that writing is a form of refuge, the principal, if not the only, vehicle for salvaging and maintaining a self.

In my concluding chapter, I focus on *The Armies of the Night*, Norman Mailer's highly praised and controversial work based on his participation in the 1967 march on the Pentagon. Of all the literary journalists discussed thus far, Mailer is most acutely aware of the precarious position of the postmodern self. Though his exhibitionist tendencies are often criticized and misunderstood, Mailer acknowledges the importance of a "performing self" in an impersonal and symbolically mediated environment that often obviates statements of personal identity. Not surprisingly, he frequently presents a combative personality defined by aggressive encounters with social others. Throughout *The Armies of the Night*, Mailer both questions what it means to be an American male in the last half of the twentieth century and articulates a self that is emblematic of this time period. His exploration of national character is frequently revealed, as it is in the writings of John McPhee, in his discussion of cultural types who embody specific values and beliefs. Though Mailer is often quick to categorize and generalize about others, he celebrates and reaffirms—as does, once again, McPhee—the myth of the imperial male self.

2

Self and the Performance of Others: The Pastoral Vision of John McPhee

After graduating from Princeton University in 1953 and doing a year of postgraduate work at Cambridge, John McPhee aspired to make a living as a freelance writer. For a time, he wrote plays for live television. Despite some success—three of his plays were sold—he felt frustrated with this kind of writing. In order to get any work done on time, McPhee found it necessary to tie himself down by threading the sash of his bathrobe through the spokes of his captain's chair. Between 1954 and 1957, he also tried, unsuccessfully, to sell ideas and finished pieces to *The New Yorker*. In 1957, however, he was hired as a staff writer at *Time* magazine, where much of his energy was devoted to writing celebrity profiles—pieces on Jackie Gleason, Sophia Loren, Joan Baez, Richard Burton, and others. Though journalism portraiture would later become the cornerstone of his work, McPhee found little satisfaction in this type of mass-magazine writing. "It was like mowing the lawn," McPhee explains. "Once a week, you had to do it. Editors would come in and say, 'How would you like to write 5,000 words on Barbra Streisand?' and I would wince. They always had you on the defensive."[1] At least part of McPhee's dissatisfaction was the result, as he suggests, of being locked into the routine patterns of organizational journalism. In his introduction to *The John McPhee Reader*, William Howarth explains that McPhee's tenure "at *Time* was lucrative, exhausting, and ultimately deadening. *Time* had a hierarchical structure; younger writers mainly did what senior editors advised."[2] Nevertheless, McPhee worked at *Time* for seven years.

In 1963, nine years after his first rejection notice, "Basketball and Beefeaters" was published by *The New Yorker.* The publication of "A Sense of Where You Are" in 1965 led to the hiring of McPhee as a staff writer at *The New Yorker.* In contrast to his situation at *Time*, the position at *The New Yorker* was a liberating one, allowing McPhee considerable autonomy in both choice of subject matter and length of the finished product.[3] William Howarth explains that

> *The New Yorker* has a first option on all of McPhee's work. He is free to choose a subject and estimate its length; the editors are equally free to criticize, accept, or reject his proposal. If rejected, he may still write the piece and sell it elsewhere. The magazine pays him quarterly advances, plus most expenses he incurs for travel.[4]

The terms of the arrangement have proved to be congenial ones; McPhee has written regularly for *The New Yorker* for almost thirty years.

McPhee has found a comfortable niche in the fact-writing tradition of the magazine, a tradition that emphasizes facts about the world rather than about the journalist. Unlike Mailer, Thompson, and Wolfe, McPhee refuses to play the role of celebrity writer, and he firmly believes that the author's presence should not detract from, or intrude upon, the story being told. For these reasons, as Barbara Lounsberry explains, McPhee "refuses to allow photographs of himself on his books."[5] McPhee may seldom place himself at center stage, and even less often does he offer seemingly superfluous material about himself; yet his work is by no means a neutral transcription of reality.[6] His unassuming presence cloaks the fact that his work reveals a great deal about McPhee as well as about his nominal, or manifest, subjects. McPhee's work, Howarth points out, "has always arisen from a personal core."[7] In *The Headmaster*, for example, though McPhee presents a detailed profile of Frank Boyden, the late headmaster at Deerfield, he chooses not to reveal that he was once a pupil at the academy. McPhee himself explains that " 'if you make a list of all the work I've ever done, and put a little mark beside things that relate to activities and interests I had before I was twenty, you'd have a little mark beside well over 90 percent of the pieces of writing. That is no accident.' "[8] McPhee's comment reveals, as we shall see, that a unified and consistent world view, linking the childhood self to the adult self, exists behind his nominally objective descriptions of the material world.

McPhee may assume, as well, the roles of limited participant, foil to more knowledgeable informants, and translator of arcane material to an intelligent but uninformed audience, but his most critical role is that of witness to his subjects' performances, which centers almost exclusively around their commitment to a job or calling. For example, McPhee follows Boyden, chronicled in the concluding chapter of *The Headmaster*, through a typical day at Deerfield Academy. McPhee's use of the profile, here and throughout his work, allows him to reveal his self by talking about others. The people who constitute McPhee's world might be rightfully understood as alter egos of McPhee, for the exploration of their world is in part a projection and reaffirmation of his personal values and beliefs. In an uncharacteristic moment of candor, McPhee (the author) identifies the bond that develops between the journalistic self and subject: "There is a lot of identification, even transformation, in the work I do—moving along from place to place, person to person, as a reporter, a writer, repeatedly trying to sense another existence and in some ways to share it."[9]

McPhee's constructed world, then, might be explained, in James Olney's terms, as a "composite metaphor," "a presentational image, or an expression, of the personality of its maker and of the meaning of his life."[10] This "image," or "expression," not only defines McPhee's place in the world but also provides both a picture of reality and framework for interpreting, verifying, and understanding it. McPhee's sense of the world, however, is not distinctively unique, as his identification with others suggests; it is a product of certain enduring values and beliefs he shares with his culture, both past and present, and is closely tied to how *The New Yorker*'s Harold Ross and William Shawn have chosen to explain and understand the world in nonfiction. The people who populate McPhee's world, moreover, are representative of a particular cultural model—the "authentic," "ideal," or "representative" American—and they are identified by a number of recognizable American character traits. As Barbara Lounsberry underscores in *The Art of Fact: Contemporary Artists of Nonfiction*, through his nonfiction characters McPhee tries to affirm imperiled nineteenth-century values—most notably, self-reliance and individualism—and "advance" the tradition of Emerson and Thoreau.[11] In revealing himself by talking about and through others, McPhee acknowledges the ideological nature of his enterprise: each journalistic occasion is an explanation, reaffirmation, and exhortation of his world view; when McPhee confirms the coherence and meaning of his own life, he also gives coherence and meaning to a real and symbolic social order. In the tradition of Ben Franklin, McPhee's model of self is a model (citizen) whom others may emulate. Irving Louis Horowitz points out that "the task of the autobiographer, whether consciously or otherwise, is to interpret to society how one should conduct the 'good' and avoid 'bad' influences of that society."[12] As we shall see, this is repeatedly suggested in the model performances of John McPhee's generalized other.

The locus of cultural reality in McPhee's work is dramatized in the lives of individuals who are shown to be absorbed in their work or professional calling. Though bureaucracies, organizations, and institutions are part of McPhee's world, individuals like the geologist David Love are able to do their work without being totally absorbed by them: "Gradually—as regional field offices have been closed and geologists have been consolidated in large federal centers in Menlo Park (California), Reston (Virginia), and Denver—Love has become vestigial in the structure of the Survey. He has resisted these bureaucratic winds even when they have been stiffer than the winds that come over the Medicine Bows."[13] In some cases, in fact, the individual is, synecdochically speaking, the institution. Frank Boyden, for example, is one of the last of the "magnanimous despots who . . . created enduring schools through their own individual energies, maintained them under their own absolute rule, and left them forever imprinted with their own personalities."[14] This is also true of environmentalist David Brower, former Sierra Club president and "quintessential Emersonian man."[15] McPhee explains that "popular assumptions to the contrary, no federal bureau is completely faceless."[16]

Brower, Love, Boyden, and others who populate McPhee's world are anything but faceless and anonymous. In fact, they may be identified as familiar and exemplary individualists—self-reliant individualists—who have lived in unresolved tension with society and figured prominently in American history and popular culture. They have a primary locus and independent reality in McPhee's work and yet exhibit an implicit Franklinian civic-mindedness. However, because McPhee interprets his subjects as individualists, only occasionally does he fully examine their relation to institutional structures—to the cultural, political, and economic realities that define humans as social beings. While McPhee's understanding of the socially integrated self is limited, he is more implicitly concerned with articulating a traditional and transcendent historical self, as his interest in craftsmanship reveals.

Above all else, McPhee's subjects are indeed expert craftspeople who demonstrate competence and an unparalleled skill that enables them to function successfully in their respective worlds, whether it be schoolmastering, tennis, basketball, cooking, or geology. Euell Gibbons, for example, is "the greatest living chef,"[17] and Henri Vaillancourt builds birch bark canoes as well as—probably better than—anyone else in the world. Edward Hoagland explains that McPhee "is preeminently a student of how people who are good at something do what they do: of craftsmanship, and people who in a private way thrive."[18] It is no hyperbole to suggest that McPhee celebrates a commitment to craftsmanship, one he shares, as a writer, with most of his subjects. Frank Boyden, Henri Vaillancourt, and others dedicate themselves unquestioningly to their work and find tremendous satisfaction in doing so. Unlike a number of social critics who write disparagingly about the conditions and meaning of work, the activity has positive connotations in McPhee's world, in part because his subjects exercise remarkable control over their craft.[19]

Henri Vaillancourt, for example, cuts his own trees, peels his own bark, makes his own tools (if necessary), and even delivers the birch canoes when completed. Despite or because of the control they exhibit, McPhee would have us believe this work has intrinsic value in itself. People not only define what they do but also are defined by doing. Work, in other words, has superordinate value in McPhee's world and virtually constitutes a secular religion that largely determines the conditions and limits of how we understand his subjects and their respective performances. Moreover, commitment to work, as Ben Franklin's autobiography underscores, is one of the principal ways in which mainstream Americans authenticate a self and determine social identity. This is evident in McPhee's conceptualization of his subjects as traditional and ideal Americans. McPhee's craftsmen and craftswomen are also preservers of a tradition and repositories of skill and knowledge. He explains, for example, that

> with a singleness of purpose that defeats distraction, Henri Vaillancourt has appointed himself the keeper of his art. He has visited almost all the other living bark-canoe makers, and he has learned certain things from the Indians. He has returned home believing, though, that he is the most skillful of them all.[20]

People like Boyden and Vaillancourt are, it is implied, a dying breed. McPhee often focuses on a subject—bark canoes, for example—that is either representative of former times or is presently being threatened by a swiftly changing (industrial) culture. His work stands as a testament to, and record of, some seldom practiced craft, activity, or lifestyle. While McPhee the authorial self does not sentimentalize such subjects or write wistfully about the past, his preoccupation with an older and more traditional America and its exemplary or model citizens suggests an idealized (pastoral), if not utopian, conception of the world.

McPhee implies, furthermore, that his subjects comprise a natural aristocracy. Their success is nominally determined by natural ability, not entitlement. Race, class, and gender are rarely important issues in

McPhee's work (the principal exception is *Levels of the Game*); they are not interpreted as either barriers or vehicles that might, respectively, obstruct or promote social and economic advancement. On the one hand, because McPhee is principally interested in conceptualizing a historical and ideal self rather than a political or social one, this may in part explain why issues of race, gender, and class are undervalued. The omission may also suggest, however, that McPhee has not adequately accounted for the tacit privileges that come with being a white, middle-class (upper middle-class) male in America. McPhee typically writes about men, of course, and celebrates the traditional masculine ideals of self-reliance, pragmatism, and staunch individualism. It is worth noting, however, that occasionally McPhee writes favorably about women: most notably, Carol Ruckdeschel in "Travels in Georgia," Anita Harris in *In Suspect Terrain*, and Patricia McConnell in "A Textbook Place for Bears."

Although race, class, and gender are minimized in McPhee's work, he lets us know that a good portion of his subjects are college-educated—indeed, many of them have graduate degrees. Yet, book learning is subordinated to practical and prolonged experience. McPhee's subjects are, as earlier indicated, expert doers; they are rarely desk-bound, and if their vocation-avocation is in part a sedentary one, McPhee emphasizes the moments when they are actively doing something. In McPhee's most recent work on geology, *Rising from the Plains*, geologist David Love explains that an increasing number of his colleagues, who have had little or no field experience, are relying solely on computers for testing hypotheses and proving theories. " 'How can you write or talk authoritatively about something,' " he asks McPhee, " 'if you haven't seen it? It isn't adequate to trust that the other guy is correct. You should be able to evaluate things in your own right.' "[21] Love's concern for first-hand experience with what he theorizes and writes about reflects McPhee's own belief in the primacy of experience. Witnessing the performances of his subjects enables McPhee the journalist to establish authority while simultaneously marveling at their ability both to perform a given task and navigate (see) their way through the world.

In building his birch bark canoes, for example, Henri Vaillancourt measures, McPhee explains, the crosspiece and the gunwales, "but that is all he would measure." In respect to the other parts of the canoe, "the only instruments Vaillancourt was using . . . were his eyes."[22] Similarly, the anonymous cook portrayed in "Brigade de Cuisine" "measures only with his eyes,"[23] as does Euell Gibbons. McPhee notes that "Gibbons mixed a batter with the flour and baking powder, and into it he put the cupful of hickory nuts and a large gob of mashed persimmons. Neither then nor as the trip continued did I ever see him measure anything, nor did he once fail in his eye for proportions or in his considerable understanding of the unstable relationships between time and flame."[24] Though McPhee rarely questions the ability or authority of his subjects, he often introduces objective measures to corroborate the expertise he observes. He simultaneously certifies his role as journalistic witness and defines himself as a foil to his expert's performance. In "A Forager," for instance, McPhee and Euell Gibbons are scouting for "wild" and edible food. "On a promising weed near the sage I found," McPhee notes, "a small fruit that resembled a yellow cherry tomato. I asked him if it was edible. 'That's a horse nettle,' Gibbons replies. 'It's deadly poisonous.' "[25] McPhee lives to tell this anecdote, of course. And in the concluding sentence, McPhee even reveals that he has gained eight ounces while Gibbons has gained two pounds. In other words, while the reader is fairly convinced that Gibbons is a highly competent wildlife forager and cook, McPhee reinforces this by introducing one of many objective and empirical measures—in this instance, a bathroom scale—that appear throughout his work.

An equally revealing moment occurs in McPhee's first book, *A Sense of Where You Are*. One afternoon, McPhee watches Bradley practice at the Lawrenceville gymnasium—the Princeton gym was being resurfaced. Bradley misses six jump shots in a row, all of them caroming off the back of the rim. He explains the problem to McPhee: " 'You want to know something? That basket is about an inch and a half low.' "[26] By that time, Bradley had made a mental adjustment and was making baskets consistently. Several weeks later, McPhee returns to the gymnasium, equipped with a tape measure, to corroborate or refute Bradley's observation, which, not surprisingly, turns out to be a fairly accurate one. The basket was one and one-eighth inches low. It is significant that McPhee not only witnesses Bradley's skill but provides an objective measure of it as well. He certifies the authority of both performer and witness, and asserts that *how* something is known is as important as *what* is known. In other words, information (or facts) has a secondary, or contingent, value; it is only meaningful (legitimated) by familiarity with the manner and method in which it is known: the use of an objective measure, in this case, within a social realistic/positivistic frame. Furthermore, since McPhee is sometimes effusive in his praise of Bradley and others, and could easily be accused of being too close to, or intimate with, his subjects, he distances himself from them and objectifies his identifications by introducing impersonal measures. In measuring and confirming performances by each subject, McPhee also authenticates his journalism performance (role) as a detached and reliable objective observer. Because McPhee links and conceals his "point of view so intimately with observed data," he establishes a literary "proof" that diverts, Kathy Smith explains, "the kind of scrutiny that accompanies the literary journalist's writing adventure when point of view and perspective become 'too' subjective."[27]

As these instances indicate, seeing has metaphorical and literal significance in McPhee's world, related not only to what McPhee's subjects know about their world but also to how they know where they are located in this world. One day, for example, McPhee observes that Bill Bradley is able to turn his back to the basket, flip the ball over his shoulder—"like a pinch of salt"[28]—and sink the shot. After playing basketball for so long, Bradley explains, " 'you develop a sense of where you are.' "[29] Because he has continuous awareness of where he is on the court, Bradley can still, figuratively speaking, see or know where he is even when he is not looking. The title of McPhee's book, *A Sense of Where You Are*, applies to both Bradley's play on the court and his life off the court. In other words, Bradley has a sense of self, purpose, and direction in life, and this is true of almost all of McPhee's admirable subjects.

When McPhee drives Fred Brown through the Pine Barrens, for example, he indicates that Brown "always knew exactly where he was going," and this is an area where "most people need to stop fairly often to study the topographic maps, for the roads sometimes come together in fantastic ganglia, and even when they are straight and apparently uncomplicated they constantly fork, presenting unclear choices between the main chance and culs de sac, of which there are many hundreds."[30] When Donald Gibbie and McPhee are looking for lobsters, McPhee explains, in *The Crofter & the Laird*, that Gibbie "obviously knew exactly where he was going."[31] Because this refrain and its variations occur so regularly in McPhee's work, these specific and contextual referents to his subjects' immediate and physical worlds contribute to a more general and metaphorical reading of McPhee's work. Though McPhee's portraits are nominally realistic, the uniformity of his characters or characterizations—as competent, skilled, and knowledgeable individuals who are always in control—establishes a pattern of association that elevates the actual, realistic world to an allegorical plane. This elevation of the actual reflects the author's own capacity for understanding any and all subjects that come within his purview.

Though McPhee's work is generally reviewed favorably, he is on occasion criticized for heroicizing his subjects, for emphasizing positive traits while minimizing less favorable ones. For example, Edward Hoagland (who is, incidentally, a devoted fan of McPhee's) attended Deerfield Academy at the same time McPhee did. He maintains that *The*

Headmaster "records all the good things that might have been said for [Boyden] and the school but few of the bad."[32] McPhee himself indicates that "if I have any regrets about my writing as a whole, it's about one or two people I've lionized."[33] This is particularly evident in the earlier portraits of Boyden and Bradley. Arguably, McPhee is less ebullient, and at times even moderately critical, in his later portraits. This might reveal McPhee's growth and development as a writer. Still, however, McPhee tends to conceptualize his subject in a positive—even ideal—way. It is my contention that he transcends realistic portraiture, though McPhee may argue otherwise, and creates a gallery of heroic selves within a context of everyday experience. In fact, the knowledge and consummate skill of his characters identify and contribute to what Kathy Smith calls "a 'master narrative' of heroism."[34]

For the sake of argument, even if McPhee were committed to portraying his subjects in a more neutral—objective—way, the nature of his journalistic occasions contribute, invariably and unavoidably, to his idealization of others. That is, it is characteristic of McPhee to contact a prospective subject and establish the "contract" of their interaction. For example, McPhee asked Euell Gibbons "if he would like to take a week or so and make a late-fall trip in central Pennsylvania living off the land."[35] McPhee establishes the context, in other words, where his subjects can showcase their particular talents. McPhee then gives them his undivided attention and they, in turn, affect a form of role-playing: acting out a familiar activity that's elevated to a performance and, more likely than not, "tainted" by the actor's awareness of the role he or she is playing. Erving Goffman explains that "when the individual presents himself before others, his performance will tend to incorporate and exemplify the officially accredited values of the society, more so, in fact, than does his behavior as a whole."[36] Because McPhee's subjects know they are being observed—often in a one-on-one situation—they arguably present themselves, as Goffman maintains, in a favorable and proper way. While a few of McPhee's later profiles may indeed reflect a commitment to authorial neutrality, they might also identify less self-conscious subjects—Henri Vaillancourt, for example—who do not conceal the discordant elements of their performances. The attention McPhee devotes to "dramaturgical discrepancies" may humanize his characters and underscore his own nominal objectivity and growth as a writer. It also makes the reader—this reader anyway—equally aware of the subject's inability to live up to or conform to McPhee's model or idealized other. Finally, for my purposes, the shared and ideal character traits, highlighted by McPhee, are more germane than nominal character differences and discrepancies. The performances of McPhee's subjects have ceremonial and ritual significance; they constitute an expressive revitalization and reaffirmation of the values of McPhee's symbolic community and a traditional American community. As we shall see in the following section, McPhee has a critical place in these communities as well.

As I have indicated, McPhee often portrays his journalistic self as student and foil to his more knowledgeable subjects. When he addresses readers as an author, however, he assumes the roles of, and identifies with, his educated counterparts. Like all his subjects, for example, McPhee shares a similar desire to know where he is (as a journalist) located in the world described by the authorial self. This is usually mentioned early in the text. For example, McPhee indicates in the first sentence of *The Pine Barrens* that he is situated in "the fire tower on Bear Swamp Hill, in Washington Township, Burlington County, New Jersey."[37] From this vantage point, he is able to see twelve miles in the distance. He goes on to describe the composition of the surrounding Jersey landscape, to the north, east, south, and west. Then at the end of a two and a half page opening paragraph, McPhee locks his attention on a specific location—"the halfway point between Boston and Richmond—the geographical epicenter of the developing megalopolis—in the northern part of the woods, about twenty miles from Bear Swamp Hill."[38] McPhee is referring to the New Jersey Pine Barrens, a 650,000 acre stretch of wilderness in which only fifteen people live in every square mile. More important than establishing the physical setting and specific subject of each work, McPhee precisely identifies where he was actually situated as a journalist. This concern, in defining specific coordinates or pinpointing the "geological epicenter of the developing megalopolis," is largely an epistemological one: knowing where he is greatly determines how something is known. The intersection of seeing and knowing (understanding) is illustrated, metaphorically, in McPhee's use of the Swamp Hill fire tower; it is both vantage point and perspective. Our understanding of the particular—the wilderness area known as the Pine Barrens—is enlarged and meaning is created when we see that it exists in close proximity to "New Jersey's central transportation corridor, where traffic of freight and people is more concentrated than it is anywhere else in the world."[39]

By establishing such reference points, McPhee is able to locate his readers in worlds that are remote and unfamiliar to them. Then he can go on to describe the setting in more depth by highlighting details and data. This frequently involves naming the world around him in a way reminiscent of Walt Whitman's cataloguing: "Eighty-four different kinds of birds breed in the Pine Barrens, not to mention the ones that make stopovers there, and the natives include Cooper's hawks, alder flycatchers, brown creepers, Henslow's sparrows, red crossbills, Baltimore orioles, green herons, black ducks, yellow-billed cuckoos, sharp-shinned hawks."[40] McPhee goes on to name approximately forty in all, half of the ornithological total. Part of his strategy is to include sufficient detail so that readers feel they have a comprehensive picture of the subject. In response to reading a selection from *Oranges*, some readers might feel, as did one of my students, that McPhee tells you everything there is to know about oranges. McPhee establishes a rhetoric of certainty by creating an illusion of completeness. McPhee's work, like much of *The New Yorker* writing, "assumes . . . its readers share its standard of meticulousness." Its detailed comprehensiveness identifies, as the preceding passage suggests, a "cosmopolitan style of knowingness that [both] flatters readers"[41] and affirms the author's journalistic authority.

More specifically, McPhee uses facts and minute details to elucidate particular worlds, not merely in an informational and ornamental way, but to constitute a way of knowing closely associated with both science and literary realism. Like the writers of social realist fiction and other forms of mimetic literature, McPhee creates a recognizable, or verisimilar, picture of the world for his readers. Though mimetic literature is correctly interpreted as a construct—a way of knowing—it is frequently misunderstood as a transparent window that frames reality and naturalizes the relation between what is known and how it is known and, thereby, encourages readers to see the world through recognizable (consensual) forms of representation. Facts contribute to this naturalization. Gaye Tuchman maintains that the emphasis on the accumulation of facts "presupposes that facts can be verified."[42] The very use of facts, in other words, implies a verifiable truth; they are representative "assertions about the world open to independent validation," Michael Schudson explains, and they stand "beyond the distorting influences of any individual's personal preferences."[43] This assumption cloaks, of course, the reality that facts, too, are validated by allegiance to rules and the concomitant procedures created for understanding them, such as the construct of "objectivity."

In McPhee's world, facts do seem to "speak" for themselves and carry an intrinsic meaning and power of their own, in part because McPhee seems to be relaying them in a balanced and unbiased way. But it is also because McPhee's concatenation of facts, as I indicated before, appears to be all-inclusive. Even though we will remember few of the forty birds McPhee catalogues, the very thoroughness of his list makes an authoritative assertion about his constructed world: it can be itemized, described, and verified by socially shared objective measures.

The following anecdote, involving David Brower, illustrates McPhee's preoccupation with objective verification. While McPhee listens to a Brower speech he is impressed with Brower's discussion of populations and the amounts of energy used by each. After the speech, he is equally interested in finding out about Brower's sources. When Brower tells McPhee that "the figures had been worked out in the head of a friend of his from data assembled 'to the best of his recollection,'"[44] McPhee steps out of his role as objective, impartial witness and reveals, somewhat uncharacteristically, that there is indeed a biased human being behind the journalistic mask: "'To the best of his *recollection*?'"[45] he asks. (The emphasis is McPhee's.) By McPhee's standards, recollection is not good enough; though a slight deviation in statistics would not alter the general meaning of Brower's rhetorical point, it seems to invalidate it for McPhee. The discordant elements in Brower's performance do not so much discredit him, however; in fact, they reveal more about the meticulousness of McPhee the journalist and person. The reader finds himself/herself in the hands of a writer who strives to be as accurate and truthful as humanly possible. Yet, truth and accuracy are always relatively determined. Brower's appeal to his audience is designed to be an emotional one; McPhee's appeal is largely rational, shareable but also affected by specific personal concerns. A commitment to objectivity, restraint, and factual accuracy all reveal dimensions of McPhee's personal and journalistic selves.

If McPhee's implicit criticism of Brower appears mild, he is uncharacteristically direct in his discussion of James Dickey and his gothic novel *Deliverance*. Perhaps nowhere else in his writing does McPhee aggressively eschew the roles of objective observer and deferential narrator and so candidly reveal and challenge, as an author and person, a world view so different from his own:

> In writing his novel, he had assembled "*Deliverance* country" from such fragments, restored and heightened in the chambers of his imagination. The canoes in his novel dived at steep angles down breathtaking cataracts and shot like javelins through white torrents among blockading monoliths. If a canoe were ten inches long and had men in it three inches high, they might find such conditions in a trout stream, steeply inclined, with cataracts and plunge pools and rushing bright water falling over ledges and splaying through gardens of rock. Dickey must have imagined something like that and then enlarged the picture until the trout stream became a gothic nightmare for men in full-sized canoes. A geologically maturer, less V-shaped stream would not have served. No actual river anywhere could have served his artistic purposes—not the Snake, not the Upper

Hudson, not even the Colorado—and least of all a river in Georgia, whose wild Chattooga, best of the state's white-water rivers, has comparatively modest rapids. The people of the *Deliverance* mountains were malevolent, opaque, and sinister. Arthur and Mammy Young.[46]

Arthur and Mammy Young, of course, are the friendly couple chronicled in McPhee's "Travels in Georgia." In another work, *The Survival of the Bark Canoe*, McPhee criticizes Dickey's canoe experience, which amounts to paddling in an overloaded canoe—packed with bourbon, bow and arrows, guitar, "and more duffel and cargo"—on a flat brown lake that rises dangerously to Dickey's knees. On the surface, it appears that Dickey's failure is based on the imaginative license he used in reconstructing a river (and its local inhabitants) in terms that are incongruous with the actual river (and river population). While Dickey's people are "malevolent, opaque, and sinister," McPhee knows them as the friendly couple, Arthur and Mammy Young, who give them—McPhee, Carol, and Sam—honey and cathead biscuits. Dickey's characters are "grotesques" who outstrip the most macabre configurations drawn by Sherwood Anderson, Flannery O'Connor, or Carson McCullers. In drawing such unsavory characters, Dickey is not merely being unflattering to the people who inhabit "*Deliverance* country"; he is tampering with reality—with how things really are—and creating a picture (myth) of the world that is at best unreliable and at worst entirely spurious. If Dickey had relied more on experience and what he actually saw, and less on imagination, McPhee seems to be saying, he would have made a more accurate picture of the river and its inhabitants. McPhee comes precariously close to suggesting—in his use of a social realistic analysis and his implicit criticism of the gothic novel—that "facts are not human statements about the world but aspects of the world itself."[47]

There is yet another reason for McPhee's criticism of Dickey. In McPhee's constructed world, sex is rarely mentioned—let alone sodomy at gun point—and murder occurs on another planet. The id, the instinctual man (woman), with its concomitant appetites, the irrational and uncontrollable urges and desires—immanent in the worlds of fantasy, dreams, and, in some instance, waking reality—are usurped, or sublimated, by McPhee's own and his subjects' commitment to ostensibly purposeful and worthwhile individual acts and tasks. McPhee's world is populated with intelligent, rational, and (for the most part) considerate people who are certainly not exploitative, let alone violent. They are almost always in control; order, balance, and harmony prevail. The kinds of people who inhabit "*Deliverance* country" are unacknowledged by McPhee; they are harsh, unforgiving people who live in a harsh, unforgiving environment. Nature is fraught with evil and danger.

McPhee's conception of nature tells a different story. The natural environment is frequently—much more often than any urban milieu—the setting for, or subject of, his journalism pieces. McPhee, of course, does not depict nature in benevolent terms, nor does his work consist of descriptions of pretty scenery. Nonetheless, he clearly feels more at ease in the wilderness, as the following passage indicates. McPhee steps out from behind his journalistic mask and reveals himself more as a human being than a writer:

> Last night, I slept nine hours. . . . Each night out here has been much the same. At home, I am lucky if I get five. Preoccupations there chase each other around and around, the strong ones fighting for the lead; and at three-thirty or four I get up and read, preferring the single track in the book to the whirling dozens in the brain. It's a chronic—or, at least, consistent—annoyance, and nights almost without exception are the same for me until I come to the woods, stretch out on the ground, and sleep nine hours.[48]

For similar reasons, McPhee has spent considerable time in the New Jersey Pine Barrens. He can escape the fast pace and congestion of New Jersey's transportation corridor by finding temporary sanctuary in the secluded woods. In *Oranges*, McPhee notes the salutary effects of being in an orange grove:

> The appeal of that world and, to even a greater extent, the relief of it had increased in my mind with each day in the groves, among other reasons simply because gas stations, Burger Queens, and shopping centers so dominate the towns of central Florida that the over-all effect on a springtime visitor can be that he is in Trenton during an August heat wave. The groves, in absolute contrast, are both beautiful and quiet, at moments eerie. I retreated into them as often as I could. To someone who is alone in the groves, they can seem to be a vacant city, miles wide and miles long.[49]

The orange groves and the Pine Barrens are semi-autonomous worlds that offer momentary respite from the pressures and patterns of living. In addition to retreating to a secluded and natural environment, McPhee frequently explores places (subjects) that are "outside of time" and seemingly unaffected by the larger social world. In *The Crofter & the Laird*, McPhee travels to the island of Colonsay to explore the native ground of his Scottish ancestors. It is a journey into the past, to a sequestered island whose dwindling population still lives in a nineteenth-century world. One native speculates whether "the twentieth century could ever completely reach Colonsay."[50] Similarly, Frank Boyden, headmaster at Deerfield Academy, has resisted influence from the outside world and maintained a "familial approach to education despite the spread of bureaucracy into institutions and industry and despite the increased size of his own school."[51] The headmaster's agelessness—he's still going strong after sixty-six years of work—contributes to the timeless quality of this anachronistic Deerfield world.

While these natural and timeless worlds have personal significance for McPhee, as subjects they might collectively be understood as manifestations of the pastoral impulse that characterizes much traditional American writing. As a writer, of course, McPhee does not spurn civilization, and wilderness is not merely an isolated area into which he temporarily escapes. Environmental issues and questions—preservation versus development, the relation of technology to nature—are prevalent themes in McPhee's writing (see *The Pine Barrens*, *Encounters with the Archdruid*, *Coming into the Country*, and others). While McPhee does write about some of the most pressing environmental concerns of his time, when we consider his fondness for wilderness and rural settings and timeless, out-of-the-way places, as well as the prototypical individuals who populate his world—individuals who are competent, trustworthy, and morally good—we enter a semi-idealized realm that reflects, more generally, McPhee the author's private vision of the world. The mundane and the reportorial—the surface layer of the text, which includes themes, nominal subjects, and so on—are elevated, in other words, to a level of understanding that is personal and, more specifically, metaphorical. McPhee's individual works may not be certifiably categorized as pastoral stories, but at times they are pastoral-like, and collectively they are closely akin to, and might be understood within the frame of, the pastoral allegory. The balance, order, and harmony of McPhee's pastoral vision provides a moment of sanctuary and escape and subtly reassures the reader that things are really all right in the world.

The order, balance, and harmony of McPhee's constructed and metaphorical world is generally reflected, as well, in the manner in which he presents his material (subject matter)—in his narrative strategies, rhetorical (literary) techniques, and prose style. For example, if conflict does occur, it is presented in a controlled and balanced manner. In *Encounters with the Archdruid*, McPhee sets David Brower, the conservationist, against three of his "natural enemies"—Charles Park, geologist and mineral engineer; Charles Fraser, developer; and Fred Dominy, United States Commissioner of Reclamation—and transplants them, respectively, to Glacier Peak Wilderness, Hilton Head Island, and the Colorado River, where they discuss questions and issues about the environment. George Roundy elaborates:

"Encounters with the Archdruid," in its final form, is at once a triumph of neutral reporting and a remarkably artificial piece of writing. McPhee manages neutrality by recording in full the views of advocates on both sides of the environmental controversy without offering an inkling of his own views. But in structuring the piece as he does, McPhee makes it a masterpiece of contrivance. Having arranged the confrontation he records, McPhee creates the same dialogue of opposites he used in "Levels of the Game." Paradoxically, however, the structural symmetry takes something of the edge off the complexity of issues raised in the piece; presenting such a tangled controversy so neatly, McPhee seems to have imposed orderliness upon it.[52]

In other words, McPhee's strategy of literary presentation softens but also identifies the conflict between characters, since they are situated in contexts where they can voice their differences. A tightly structured and controlled form, however, frames our reading of the text and may preempt or defuse the content as the principal means for understanding it. While the central thematic issues of *Encounters* are characterized by differing points of view—that is, by conflict—the symmetrical presentation of ideas and arguments suggests that the world McPhee describes is one really characterized by balance, harmony, and control.

Generally, I must also emphasize, McPhee's writing is characterized by a fine balance of narration and exposition, anecdotes and factual material. A character study is usually one of the unifying elements of his work. Though dialogue is employed sparingly, there is enough to develop scene and character. McPhee's less successful work usually suffers from overemphasizing one or more of the above strategies. For instance, regardless of McPhee's mastery of the subject of geology, *In Suspect Terrain* is adulterated by an overwhelming amount of technical terms. Often only after reading one of McPhee's lesser works does the reader realize how sucessfully he constructs his world without calling attention to its constituent elements; it is wrought out of a rich variety and balance of techniques, strategies, and practices.

One of the most critical ways McPhee establishes balance and internal harmony results from his ability to identify so completely with both his subjects and reading audience. Wayne C. Booth explains that "in any reading experience there is an implied dialogue among author, narrator, the other characters, and the reader. Each of the four can range, in relation to each of the others, from identification to complete opposition, on any axis of value, moral, intellectual, aesthetic, and even physical."[53] The degree of identification dramatically influences our response to the nominal subject and largely determines how we interpret the author's vision (version) of the world. For the sake of clarification, it will be useful to compare McPhee's work to that of another notable literary journalist, Hunter S. Thompson. Generally speaking, McPhee the writer does not create a literary persona that is remarkably distinct from McPhee the person and journalist; in other words, the author, narrator, and character (journalist) are similar. In much of Thompson's work, however—and this is also true of Mailer's *The Armies of the Night*—the narrator is actively antagonistic toward himself (as a character), his readers, and other characters (people) within the work. This lack of identification in Thompson's writings, not surprisingly, corresponds to his projected metaphor of self as a putative outsider or rebel who lives in open, unresolved tension with society. In McPhee's work, on the contrary, we can see an intense identification between the narrator-participant and his subjects. McPhee reveals, as I indicated earlier, who he is by talking about others. This identification is completed, so to speak, in McPhee's communication with a reading audience identified by values and beliefs that are similar to those shared by McPhee and his admirable subjects. This identification in McPhee's work—between author, narrator, character, and reader—reflects and helps determine the general balance and internal harmony of McPhee's constructed world.

McPhee, furthermore, does not indulge in literary pyrotechnics or purposely call attention to his prose. His style is invariably a modulated one, appropriate for conveying, rather than competing with, the subject being explored; it is unobtrusive, functional, and very compatible with McPhee's own place in the world: in the background. Though we know that any written picture about the world is symbolically mediated through language, McPhee's style seems to be a natural extension of the subject matter. "The photolike realism of McPhee's writing scenes . . . tends to divert any uncertainty about the authenticity of the subject. The match between image and representation tends to be regarded as natural and true to the extent that" it "offers a coherent sum of images."[54] This is the language of Realist literature which, Terry Eagleton explains,

> tends to conceal the socially relative or constructed nature of language: it helps to confirm the prejudice that there is a form of "ordinary" language which is somehow natural. This natural language gives us reality "as it is": it does not—like

Romanticism or Symbolism—distort it into subjective shapes, but represents the world to us as God himself might know it.[55]

In other words, style is not merely ornamental embellishment, a tag that distinguishes one writer from another; rather, it unobtrusively shapes and reflects the manner in which the writer, John McPhee, apprehends and makes sense of a personal and material world.

McPhee's world, as I have indicated, is populated with experts who are particularly adept in their work, profession, or vocation. They are not part of a specific socio-economic group, but their consuming interest in an activity or discipline, as well as a commitment to craftsmanship and self-reliance (among other attributes), bind them together as a distinct suprasocial unit. While a writer like "Wolfe is habitually speaking *through* his subjects, using them as media. . . . McPhee is the medium through which his subjects speak." But both writers, nonetheless, "manipulate the voice of the subject to legitimize their own authorial acts"[56] and interests. As I noted, McPhee is interested in a group made up of people who share many of his own values and beliefs. He focuses on a particular dimension of their lives and work and represents the self, as I suggested, as a recognizable type or model. McPhee's "characters" are no mere facsimiles of each other, of course; he celebrates uniqueness in each while he conceptualizes each life as one commitment to the common model of the authentic or representative (male) American. One shared belief among these archetypes, McPhee has us believe, is their commitment to the primacy of actual everyday experience. At a time when the material world has for many readers lost its immediacy, and we live increasingly in a symbolically mediated, often hazily understood environment, McPhee's subjects make contact with and reaffirm a relation to the natural and immediate physical world. McPhee itemizes and presents pictures of this common world by presenting information that is understandable to the interested reader. Thus McPhee acts on the belief that knowledge is the provenance of all people. He constructs an informed and competent reader who shares in a democratic epistemology that is revealed in a community of generalized and ideal others.

3

Joe McGinniss' *Fatal Vision*: The Search for an Anti/Heroic Self

While it took John McPhee over two decades to establish himself as one of America's preeminent writers of literary nonfiction, Joe McGinniss achieved success at a much younger age. After graduating from Holy Cross in 1964—the same year McPhee was writing *A Sense of Where You Are*, his first book of nonfiction—McGinniss worked as a reporter at the *Port Chester Daily Item* until he found an evening berth, nine months later, on the *Worchester Telegram*. In the following year, 1965, he fulfilled one of his life ambitions by becoming a sportswriter for the *Philadelphia Bulletin*. Soon afterward, editors at the *Philadelphia Inquirer*—the *Bulletin*'s principal rival—offered McGinniss a job as a sports columnist. He turned it down and audaciously requested a position as a general issues columnist. The proposal was accepted by the *Inquirer*'s editorial staff, and McGinniss, at age twenty-four, became the youngest columnist for a major U.S. newspaper. While McGinniss initially focused his triweekly pieces on subjects of local interest, within twelve months he was reporting on current and often controversial issues and events of national importance. It was a column on the assassination of Robert F. Kennedy that eventually contributed to his departure from the newspaper. When McGinniss wrote that the senator's death was an indirect result of a violent American society, the *Inquirer*'s conservative publisher, Walter H. Annenberg, issued a public apology (editorial) that so incensed the young journalist that he took a leave of absence to complete an interview with Howard Cosell for *TV Guide*.

McGinniss learned from one of Cosell's acquaintances that Richard Nixon and Hubert Humphrey had hired Madison Avenue advertising agencies to direct their media campaigns. He was so interested in the idea of getting a behind-the-scenes look into the world of created (political) images that he quit his job at the *Philadelphia Inquirer* and spent five months with the Nixon campaign doing the kind of in-depth "legwork" Tom Wolfe has described as "saturation reporting." McGinniss sat in on staff "brainstorming" sessions, was privy to the tapings of panel shows and political commercials, and regularly interviewed Nixon's top media consultants. McGinniss' efforts resulted in the publication of *The Selling of the President 1968*, a book that spent seven months on the best-seller list—four months at the top—and appeared in the same year, 1969, as Joan Didion's *Slouching Towards Bethlehem*, James Simon Kunen's *The Strawberry Statement*, and John McPhee's *Levels of the Game*. With the exception of Anne Frank, McGinniss, at age twenty-seven, was the youngest writer of nonfiction to have authored such a popular and critically acclaimed book. McGinniss would go on to write about this early success in *The Dream Team*—an autobiographical first novel about a young, acclaimed writer on a book-promoting tour—and in his second work of nonfiction, *Heroes*.[1]

The Selling of the President 1968 appeared at a critical juncture in American life. In a decade filled with a seemingly endless number of highly visual and significant events—mass demonstrations and the Vietnam War to name just two—the media, particularly television, played an increasingly prominent role in reporting news and shaping our understanding of social and political realities. While the importance of the television was indisputable, the use (or abuse) of the medium was a subject of considerable debate—and concern. The most recognized (quoted) media guru of the decade was Marshall McLuhan. If he implicitly endorsed a media technocracy in his discussion of a global community, other social critics, including McGinniss, contended that television created a symbolic world of images that threatened to transform our lives by replacing everyday realities with manufactured ones: "The televised image, McGinniss maintains in *The Selling of the President 1968*, "can become as real to the housewife as her husband, and much more attractive."[2]

Though McGinniss defines his journalistic role as a seemingly objective witness—observing people and events rather than judging them—*The Selling of the President 1968* is a vivid illustration of the muckraking journalism that reached popular acceptance in the 1970s with the publication of *All the President's Men* (1974) and the founding of *Mother Jones* (1976). McGinniss' intention is to reveal the disparity between the created image and the reality it allegedly represents. A naive public may think that Richard Nixon was a new person in 1968; McGinniss underscores, however, that he was very similar to the person who was defeated by JFK in the 1960 presidential election. In fact, it was only Nixon's image—"redesigned in keeping with the McLuhanesque realities of a television-addicted electorate"[3]—that had been transformed. The Nixon campaign is one example, according to McGinniss, of how television can be used to sell political candidates much in the same way advertisers sell consumer products. While television may indeed present images that do not correspond to a shared and objectively identifiable social reality, McGinniss implicitly constructs an audience whose members are allegedly powerless in their ability to distinguish reality from created images. Being a writer who has a "powerful aversion" to this often-maligned medium, McGinniss seems to regret that the advent of television fostered a new form of cultural expression that increased the importance of images at the expense of the written word.

McGinniss' criticism of television reveals, moreover, a more implicit personal and cultural concern centering on the erosion of values and myths associated with a more idealized American past. In *The Selling of the President 1968*, for example, McGinniss explores, as he does in all of his works of nonfiction, the model of the heroic self—or culturally ideal character—in a society that so readily embraces celebrities and public figures. McGinniss more specifically maintains that political candidates are no longer measured against their "predecessors—not against a standard of performances established by two centuries of democracy—but against Mike Douglas."[4] Since in the last half-century the old heroic mold has been broken, Americans increasingly depend on "pseudo-events" and the celebration of public personalities to assuage their " 'exaggerated expectations of human greatness.' "[5] In this context, Richard Nixon represents, according to McGinniss, a new category of human emptiness: an unethical, ambitious, and characterless figure who relied on television to both create a more favorable image and shield himself from a constituency he secretly disdained and to which he felt superior. While this image of our thirty-seventh president may be shared by many Americans in the aftermath of Watergate, Richard Nixon is also an emblematic figure in McGinniss' journalistic world; the failure and flaws of our former national leader are representative of the moral and spiritual poverty of the American citizenry.

Though McGinniss' works bear little resemblance to the work of another popular nonfiction writer, Gay Talese—author of *The Bridge* (1965), *The Kingdom and the Power* (1969), *Honor Thy Father* (1971), and *Thy Neighbor's Wife* (1980)—they both share a deep and abiding interest in family relationships. Barbara Lounsberry explains that Talese "tends to be drawn obsessively toward the parent-child relation. In his work he expands the specific dilemma of how to honor one's father in a changing age to the larger question of how to honor the national spirit, the American dream of our *forefathers*, in a similarly changing and diminished era."[6] In *The Selling of the President 1968* and other works of nonfiction—*Heroes* (1976), *Going to Extremes* (1980), *Fatal Vision* (1983), and *Blind Faith* (1988)—McGinniss reveals a similar preoccupation with real and symbolic figures of authority, often fathers. Though the father-son relationships Talese writes about tell a story of his own life—a "story of a son" who fails "to live up to his father's expectations"[7]—the works of both McGinniss and Talese have more general social relevance in an era when challenging authority, particularly patriarchal authority, has redefined many father-son relationships. For this and other reasons, "the individual psychodramas of Talese's subjects"—and this is often true of McGinniss' as well—might be interpreted as the "national psychodramas of us all."[8]

If throughout his collected works McPhee articulates and affirms a series of ideal selves within contexts of everyday experience, McGinniss repeatedly underscores how figures of authority and other allegedly model types fail to measure up to archetypal or culturally determined standards of heroism and success. Like McPhee, McGinniss often relies on journalism portraiture and focuses on the lives of individuals—often individualists—who embrace representative male American values and conform to culturally prescribed roles and modes of behavior. McGinniss probes beneath the surface, or facade, of personal and social realities, as he does in *The Selling of the President 1968*, and exposes the gap in American life between its expressed ideals and its reality. In both his choice of subject matter and in highly personal reading of various social worlds, McGinniss stamps his own image—vision—on the face of reality and creates, as we shall see in *Heroes*, a metaphorical and self-oriented world that intersected with specific patterns of American life in the 1970s.

Heroes was published during a period of American life when disenchantment with authority was perhaps deeper and more widespread than at any other time in our history. While this crisis was most evident throughout the 1960s in the adversarial culture's rejection of parental authority and mainstream politics, it culminated in, and was symbolized by, the Watergate investigation and the eventual resignation of Richard Nixon. It may be an overstatement to suggest that the country was traumatized by this failure in its national leadership. This highly significant and symbolic historical event, however, did not necessarily lead to the demystification of authority and the establishment of a more democratic society and conscientious public. In fact, in some instances feelings of personal dislocation led either to joining a cult or establishing an idolatrous relationship with other authoritative and often suspect charismatic leaders. A considerable number of other Americans found personal and secular "salvation" in the therapeutic quest for physical or psychological well-being. In *Heroes*, these two patterns are intertwined in McGinniss' attempt to overcome personal emptiness and discontent through a search for, and identification with, the vanishing American hero.

Heroes is composed of a series of sketches and profiles of prominent and celebrated cultural figures: Edward Kennedy, Senator (and former astronaut) John Glenn, William C. Westmoreland, Eugene McCarthy, and, among others, Congressional Medal of Honor winner Joe Hooper. McGinniss initially sees his subjects as ideal figures and plans to talk to them about the role of the hero in contemporary American life. Periodically throughout *Heroes* McGinniss also provides impressionistic glimpses into his own troubled life. He is estranged from his first wife and involved in another difficult relationship. He drinks excessively, as do a number of his subjects. More generally, McGinniss reveals an implicit preoccupation with childhood and youth and laments that he cannot live eternally in the aura of his earlier success—being a well-known author at age twenty-seven.

Part of McGinniss' agenda is to come to terms with his loss by talking to other once-celebrated figures about their former accomplishments and successes. When he meets with former presidential candidate Eugene McCarthy, for example, McGinniss intends to ask him what it is like to no longer be at the center of important events. Instead, however, McGinniss lapses into a private conversation with himself—and the reader—and acknowledges that while he had written a best-selling work of nonfiction, part of him "needed to not succeed."[9] McGinniss' personal problems and fear of success are underscored by his desire to be close to, or recognized by, others who have succeeded; he explains, for example, that he "wanted to feel a closeness to [William] Styron, a degree of intimacy, a sense of shared experience" and, "mostly, to feel *accepted* by Styron because . . . I thought that might make me more acceptable to myself."[10] While in this and other confessional moments McGinniss often reveals aspects of his personality by talking about, even identifying with, his journalistic subjects, he is unable to achieve critical distance from the self and frequently lapses into moments of narcissistic self-absorption. The brevity of his portraits and vignettes, furthermore, prevents him from fully examining the role of the modern hero and linking an introspective, private self to the collective (social) identity of his subjects. McGinniss may successfully reconstruct scenes and skillfully employ revealing dialogue, as he does throughout *The Selling of the President 1968*, but his quest for the American hero is invariably subverted because he either sees his own unheroic self mirrored in the world around him or places his subjects in contexts in which they can only be average American citizens. For instance, McGinniss records in considerable detail the amount of alcohol he consumes, and he makes readers equally aware that some of his subjects—Joe Hooper and William Styron to name just two—have an appetite commensurate with his own. And after visiting an evening with John Glenn, McGinniss concludes his brief, page-and-a-half profile by saying "no matter how hard I tried to resist, the less he [Glenn] seemed like the first American to have orbited the earth and the more he seemed like the next junior senator from Ohio."[11] McGinniss identifies Glenn's earlier heroics as an astronaut and then unfairly condemns him, I believe, for being merely human, a junior senator who could never live up to the author's mythic standards of heroism. McGinniss believes that we live in a time when there is little or nothing to be heroic about. Whether or not this is an accurate assessment of American life in the last half of the twentieth century is less important than the realization that "all human possibility seems tarnished," as literary critic Ronald Weber points out, because of the author's own "sense of personal failure."[12] McGinniss' own experiences and personality traits, his biases and personal preoccupations and problems, influence his interpretation of the nonfiction subject matter and invariably shape the book's final vision by investing it with his distinctive—and often pessimistic—world view.

McGinniss suggests that his personal problems and crises are the result of a troubled family life. He periodically reenters his past and provides information relevant to our understanding of the adult author. Like Joan Didion, as we shall see later, McGinniss often presents these moments of self-disclosure in a candid, even confessional manner: "Here are some things about me which possibly you should know,"[13] he announces to the reader. McGinniss goes on to reveal that he was a "skinny, awkward, weak, and physically uncourageous"[14] child who lived a "splendid fantasy life" by inventing complicated sports games played with dice.[15] McGinniss' picture of his unheroic self is implicitly explained by, and mirrored in, an equally unheroic portrait of his alcoholic and frequently absent father, a quiet clumsy man resented by his son because he did not know how to be a father (i.e. masculine). McGinniss also reveals that he was the only child of a forty-year-old mother who had miscarried twice before. At a very young age he was made aware "that it would be almost exclusively by my words, my actions, and my fate that my mother's happiness, or lack of it, would be determined."[16] McGinniss' quest for the American hero appears in part to be a therapeutic search for more acceptable parental (authoritative) figures—particularly a surrogate father—with whom he can identify and by whom he can be accepted. Instead of selecting more appropriate models, or at least identifying positive character traits as McPhee does with his subjects, McGinniss endows these potentially ideal figures with problems—most notably, excessive drinking—that approximate his father's (and his own) shortcomings. McGinniss inadvertently projects his problems onto symbolic others and affirms his fragile ego and unheroic identity by aligning himself with a community of similar, and often flawed, individuals. Because McGinniss seems intent on recreating and affirming this childhood dependence, it invariably prevents him from acknowledging responsibilities and presenting a more autonomous adult self. In fact, periodically throughout *Heroes* McGinniss all but states—perhaps in part to deflect criticism by announcing his shortcomings—that he acts irresponsibly, even immaturely. He left his wife and children, as I noted, and is currently living with photographer Nancy Doherty. He is petulant, moody, self-centered. When Nancy is present he is not interested in her, and when she is away—in some instances driven away—McGinniss wants her back to stem his loneliness and provide comfort and security.

Early on in the work McGinniss takes Nancy to a summer camp in the Catskill Mountains where he "had spent seven happy summers as a boy."[17] The camp closed two years before their visit and the cabins are now falling to ruin: windows are broken and paint peels from the walls as the roofs slowly deteriorate. McGinniss' connection to this idealized world of childhood is as tenuous as the cabins' slipping cinder-block foundations. As they take a symbolic walk through his irrecoverable past, McGinniss shows Nancy a cabin where he had written his name in shoe polish almost twenty years earlier. As they leave the camp grounds, McGinniss explains to the reader that "I felt not only sadness. I felt fear. I decided I would have to keep Nancy with me a while longer."[18] Another chapter is devoted to the funeral of McGinniss' best friend Peter. McGinniss spends most of the three pages recounting experiences of their younger years and implicitly suggests that a certain part of his own life—his adolescence and more carefree days—was laid to rest when his friend was buried. In these two revealing autobiographical moments, McGinniss is unable to reconcile his present life with the past because he retreats, perhaps unintentionally, into a symbolic childhood world; his desire "to keep Nancy with" him "a while longer" identifies a self-centered dependency on a "nurturing" figure who can temporarily allay his feelings of loss, sadness, and fear.

While McGinniss might confront his experiences and recreate a more meaningful identity by linking an examined self to his quest for the vanishing American hero, he seems principally intent on confessing shortcomings and inadvertently wallowing in a mire of personal problems. McGinniss' subject could be a promising one, but it "is so fragmented and is carried out on such a superficial level," Ronald Weber points out, "it is hard to believe he has more than passing interest in it."[19] The cumulation of his collage-like entries—brief profiles, random comments about the contemporary hero, information about his past, columns written when he was at the *Philadelphia Bulletin*—doesn't make for a significantly meaningful pattern as it does in, say, Hunter S. Thompson's *Hell's Angels*, a multi-perspective, anti-hierarchical account of the notorious outlaw motorcycle gang. Not surprisingly, McGinniss' conclusion only underscores the problems evident throughout *Heroes*. He unconvincingly—and superficially—suggests that we can no longer live "with prefabricated myths." We can only construct our own, "slowly, painfully, piece by piece." For McGinniss, this centers on writing: "Writing about the loss of illusions—the vanishing of heroes—can compensate, in however small and unsatisfactory a way," he explains, "for the no longer deniable fact that they are gone."[20] While McGinniss nominally concludes his personal and cultural quest for the vanishing American hero, in this third and most significant work of literary nonfiction, *Going to Extremes*, he continues, once again, this metaphorical search, though in a less self-conscious (and self-indulgent) way.

Whether it was journalistic instinct, personal interest, or opportunism, McGinniss selected a subject—the "country" of Alaska—that had a fairly widespread appeal to an American reading audience. Following the success of McPhee's *Coming into the Country* (1977)—his first national bestseller—McGinniss' work was published in the early 1980s, and it helped re-establish the reputation he had lost with his two previous works, *The Dream Team* and *Heroes*. Unlike his previous work of literary nonfiction, McGinniss presents his journalist self in a more modest fashion in *Going to Extremes*. In fact, while the book is once again a personal journey, narrated in the first person, McGinniss rarely offers information about his own life and frequently casts himself as a detached observer, much as John McPhee does, who is chiefly interested in talking to and recording the experiences of other (transplanted) Americans. McGinniss does reveal, however, that he had become increasingly interested in the subject of Alaska over the two previous years. And because he had spent most of this time "cooped up inside a stuffy little workroom in New Jersey . . . writing a book [*Heroes*] that had turned out to be mostly about the inside of" his head, he "was hungry for something different: something big, something fresh, something new. Like Alaska."[21] He explains, furthermore, that he wanted to experience and write about what might "be the last days of the last frontier America would ever have."[22] While McGinniss offers only these brief explanations, it is evident that his personal odyssey—escape from confining, civilized space into unfamiliar and semi-unchartered wilderness—invokes a pattern of writing, the journey narrative, which has been a characteristic expression in American life for several hundred years. As the last American frontier, McGinniss also transforms this culturally significant landscape into a metaphorical and personally meaningful setting in which the author can once again pursue his quest for the heroic self, or the model of the vanishing American frontiersman.

McGinniss travels extensively throughout Alaska; he begins his journey from Seattle in November and ends the following summer with a wilderness hike through the Brooks Range in Northern Alaska. McGinniss visits Fairbanks, Anchorage, and Juneau (the state capital), as well as a number of smaller towns, villages, and settlements—such as Point Barrow at the northern-most tip of Alaska—which are often sparsely populated and isolated by large tracts of wilderness. It would be an overstatement to suggest that Alaska is, for McGinniss, a ground for anarchic freedom. Instead of committing himself to an in-depth examination of some aspect of Alaskan life, however, he chooses an itinerary that allows for considerable journalistic and personal freedom. When McGinniss at times feels "trapped" by one of his experiences, as I will discuss later, he can pack his bag and head off, as it were, to new territory. While McGinniss is certainly adept at describing the geographical and cultural "landscapes" of Alaska, his inability to remain rooted for an extended period of time at least partially undermines his purported commitment to local-color writing. McGinniss' work affirms the value of traveling itself, quite apart from his ostensible goals, and despite that, a successful book resulted from his journey. Moreover, since traveling and travel writing have typically been a masculine prerogative, this type of journey constitutes a kind of personal and social transcendence realized in an escape from both restrictive journalistic conventions and in-depth commitment to people who have lives outside the specific subject-author encounter.

Though McGinniss rarely focuses in great depth on a particular individual, a series of highly revealing profiles is the central core of *Going to Extremes*. Like McPhee, McGinniss seems to believe that the locus of cultural understanding is most ideally expressed in the lives of individuals. Many of McGinniss' characters are, in effect, embodiments of the authentic American—or American Adam—but in an adulterated form. This mythic and ideal figure has traditionally been defined in positive terms: as independent, self-reliant, opportunistic, uncorrupt and fundamentally innocent. While McPhee's subjects are facsimiles of this cultural model, in McGinniss' metaphorical world people seem incapable, generally speaking, of embracing and living up to these ideals. McGinniss is drawn to quirky, unstable and marginal figures—lives often replete with problems—who represent the underside of the frontier experience. "Unlike most other literary journalists," Linda Steiner explains, "McGinniss tends not to develop or sustain affection for the people and cultures he describes. His intense negativism, if not hostility, brings him closer to the bleak worldview of some modern novelists and separates him from the more tolerant or even enthusiastic sensibility of [some] literary journalists."[23]

On the ferry ride from Seattle to Alaska, which opens the book, McGinniss introduces us, for example, to a woman named Sandy, who tells the author her life story. She grew up in Hastings, Nebraska. When she turned eighteen, at the end of the 1960s, she headed for California. After discovering that the "action" was no longer in California, she drifted up the coast to San Francisco, Portland, Eugene, Seattle and finally ended up in Juneau, Alaska. She found a job with the state legislature and was soon using cocaine, drinking excessively—ten or twelve beers a night—and sleeping with a number of men, including her boyfriend's work partner. While Sandy is described as a person with her own identity, albeit a troubled one, her personal story is not unlike the stories of many other transplanted Alaskans. Sandy's journey West, which eventually leads to Alaska—the last frontier and a place of opportunity—is emblematic of the trip made by countless other Americans, present and past, who sought a new life and identity as well as a place of refuge in which they could escape from a troublesome and/or confining past. McGinniss explains, for example, that before Ted Healy became a principal at Barrow High School in Barrow, Alaska, he had been an assistant principal in Eureka, California. And "like so many other Alaskans and, particularly, like so many other whites in Barrow," he "had recently been divorced. Barrow had seemed as clean a break with his past as he could make."[24] McGinniss' profiles, here and throughout much of the book, invoke, update, and challenge our country's foundation myth by creating a contemporary and metaphorical landscape that neither idealizes nor elegizes, as is often the case in popular literature and film, a frontier world so often associated with American progress and expansionism.

One of the most dramatic and ostensibly revealing moments occurs when McGinniss attends a dinner party at the house of a Barrow High

School instructor. After more than one round of drinks, one of the guests, Wade Smith, stands abruptly, hurls his glass against the floor, and starts to yell as he charges the host. " 'Seven-thirty! Seven-thirty! It's already seven-thirty and now you're just starting to cook dinner.' " As some of the guests try to restrain him, he shouts: " 'You know I eat dinner at six o'clock! You miserable, flatulent son of a bitch. You overweight mongoloid bastard.' " He tells the host that he plans never to return to his house again—as if the host would invite him back—and then informs his wife that if she does not leave with him immediately that she is "a disloyal harlot and a slut and that he would go home and load his rifle and shoot her through the forehead the minute she walked in the door."[25] Then he slaps her across the face before several of the guests push him out the door. Everyone eventually sits down to a meal of baked potatoes, onions, corn, Olympia beer, and fried caribou steak. Midway through dinner, McGinniss hears a plane coming into Barrow, which will leave, he knows, for Anchorage within an hour. He explains to the reader that "suddenly it seemed that I had been in Barrow half my life." He announces to the others at the dinner table that he had to get on that plane. "No one asked why. Everyone understood," McGinniss explains. "They would all have gone, too, if they'd been able."[26]

Prior to describing this memorable evening, McGinniss tells the reader—in part as an explanation for Wade Smith's behavior and his own unceremonious departure—that the "whites of Barrow found themselves, as winter closed in, forced into strange, tense, dependent relationships with one another,"[27] and that the Smith family's three-year stay in Barrow was unusually long for white people. While McGinniss acknowledges that an unusual degree of psychological stability was necessary to survive in Alaska—and most people "displayed an extraordinary absence of the same"[28]—he articulates an environmental determinism that not only shapes and is an explanation for human behavior but implicitly and in part exonerates people of their moral and social responsibilities. McGinniss acknowledges that there is indeed an important psychological component to living in Alaska. Generally, however, he only describes manifestations of this in idiosyncratic behavior—as he does in the example of Wade Smith—and seldom, if ever, attempts to probe or chronicle the spiritual or psychological reality of his subjects—or himself. His subjects are typically "bored, cynical; they abuse drink, drugs, each other. McGinniss refuses to become intimate with any of them. Consequently, his vignettes are precise but cursory. His writing is informed by his moral position, but not by any high degree of intensity or sense of spiritual possibility."[29]

McGinniss' sudden departure underscores his point that the oppressive environment—bitterly cold weather and extended periods of darkness—can make almost any stay in Barrow (and other parts of Alaska) too long. It also reminds the reader that he is a journalist who temporarily forsakes his participatory role—when experiences are too unpleasant—and underscores that he is ill-suited for certain aspects of frontier life. In a similar and equally revealing autobiographical moment, McGinniss decides that he is going to spend three days and three nights in a wilderness cabin at Crescent Lake—without alcohol, books, magazines, and other amenities of "civilized" life. Not surprisingly, McGinniss is just short of miserable, and, to his credit, he does not hide this from the reader. His brief frontier "test" may be a failure—McGinniss is no frontier hero—but he successfully transforms this experience in writing by casting himself as Everyman and telling his story from the perspective with which middle-class, educated readers can vicariously identify without feeling threatened by their own lack of heroic ideals.

While McGinniss is indeed the focus, or subject, of the aforementioned event, much more often than not he subordinates his journalistic presence, as both participant and writer, and lets others speak for themselves as they might in a work of oral history. McGinniss regularly lets his subjects speak for paragraphs, even pages, uninterrupted. At times this seems like an evasion of authorial responsibility, merely a transcription of tape-recorded stories and conversations. As in other works of literary journalism, however—Michael Herr's *Dispatches* and Hunter S. Thompson's *Hell's Angels*, for example—McGinniss constructs a more democratic mode of discourse by focusing on the lives of average (common) people and playing down his journalistic authority while minimizing the role that public spokespersons—politicians and government officials, for example—often play in shaping journalistic content. McGinniss locates cultural interpretation in reciprocal contexts and implicitly underscores that reality is a product—and process—negotiated between multiple subjects. McGinniss orchestrates, usually successfully, a full range of voices, but his commitment to inclusiveness often precludes longer, more in-depth profiles and unavoidably prevents us from seeing his subjects as individuated selves. Moreover, while McGinniss' subjects are often individualists, he does not necessarily portray them as individuals. In fact, their principal value in McGinniss' reimagined literary world depends less on their personal differences than the author's implicit commitment to his model of the heroic/anti-heroic self. If McPhee's work is an affirmation of what is best in the lives of model Americans, *Going to Extremes* underscores that not only is

America's final frontier closing but there are precious few heroic Americans, including McGinniss himself, capable of filling the role of the traditional and idealized frontiersman (or frontierswoman).

In McGinniss' following two works of creative nonfiction, *Fatal Vision* (1983) and *Blind Faith* (1989), he returns to the lower forty-eight and explores another distinctly American "terrain": the murder/crime story. Once again McGinniss selected a subject that has had enduring and immense appeal to a large reading audience. In addition to such canonical works as Norman Mailer's *The Executioner's Song* (1979) and Truman Capote's *In Cold Blood* (1965), which helped legitimate not only the New Journalism but the murder/crime genre as well, other best-selling works—Joseph Wambaugh's *The Onion Field* (1973) and Vincent Bugliosi's *Helter Skelter* (1975), to name just two—appeared years before the popular success of McGinniss' books. All of these works were produced as either Hollywood films or made-for-TV movies. The American public's morbid fascination with these gruesome tales culminated in Jonathan Demme's *The Silence of the Lambs*. The film's central character, Dr. Hannibal "The Cannibal" Lecter, is romanticized for his intellect and overpowering physical (screen) presence while simultaneously and somewhat paradoxically portrayed as a monster who dines not on lamb chops but human flesh—uncooked, of course.

The central characters (and murderers) of McGinniss' *Fatal Vision* and *Blind Faith*—respectively, Dr. Jeffrey MacDonald and Robert Marshall—are neither insane nor psychopathic, but like Dr. Hannibal "The Cannibal" Lecter they exhibit a charismatic power—superficial as it may be—that veils and in part explains their self-centered, ambitious, and destructive natures. In *Fatal Vision*, McGinniss constructs, in exacting (and at times repetitive) detail, the tribulation—and trials—of a young doctor who appears to be an all-American boy unjustly accused of murdering his wife, Colette, and their two daughters, Kimberly and Kristen. In high school he had been king of the senior prom and quarterback of the football team, as well as student council president. His graduating class voted him Most Popular and Most Likely to Succeed. He went to college at Princeton University and then completed his education at Northwestern University Medical School. He married his attractive high school sweetheart and even enlisted in the Army and trained to be a Green Beret. This all-American dream turned into an American tragedy—and nightmare—on February 17, 1970 when MacDonald woke up on the bedroom floor of his apartment on the Fort Bragg, North Carolina Army base and discovered that his family had been brutally stabbed and clubbed to death. MacDonald told authorities that three men and one woman, dressed in hippy attire, had entered the apartment and killed his family while they chanted "Kill the Pigs" and "Acid is Groovy." With the exception of superficial injuries—minor flesh wounds and a bump on the head—MacDonald miraculously survived the attack. Early on in the investigation, the Army's Criminal Investigation Division (CID) compiled evidence that pointed to MacDonald as their chief suspect. The case was eventually dismissed, however, because the Army's CID investigation was, to put it kindly, mishandled and fraught with mistakes. MacDonald went public with his story (of innocence) and even appeared on "The Dick Cavett Show." While MacDonald clearly enjoyed this public attention, and was quickly adjusting to bachelorhood, Fred and Mildred Kassab, Colette's parents, were interested in finding the people who killed their daughter and grandchildren. Up to this point, Kassab believed unequivocally in his son-in-law's innocence. Once Kassab received a copy of the report compiled by the Army's Criminal Investigation Division, however, he came to the conclusion that MacDonald was the murderer, and he then devoted several years of his life in an effort to have his son-in-law tried again. Ten years after the death of his wife and children, MacDonald was brought to trial in a federal court in Raleigh, North Carolina and convicted of second degree murder in the deaths of Kimberly and Colette and first degree murder in the death of Kristen, his youngest daughter. He was sentenced to three life terms in prison, to be served consecutively (not concurrently).

Not surprisingly, McGinniss' book became a best-seller, and before a word was written he received a $300,000 advance from Dell/Delacorte publishing company. Despite that MacDonald received 26.5 percent of the advance as well as 33 percent of all royalties, he was not pleased with the finished product. Expecting a book that would depict him favorably and serve as a vehicle to extol his innocence, MacDonald felt betrayed by McGinniss' negative portrayal and filed a lawsuit against the author for fraud and breach of contract. MacDonald believed that McGinniss had violated a contract to uphold and document, in a positive way, his life story, which McGinniss had learned by spending many hours with his subject. Their relationship began when MacDonald asked McGinniss to stay with him and his defense team during the murder trial. MacDonald gave the author privileged access to his personal files and later sent McGinniss taped-recorded messages and numerous letters from prison. "In turn," Linda Steiner explains, "McGinniss wrote MacDonald a series of friendly, encouraging, supportive letters; this correspondence never hints that McGinniss had come to believe the prosecutors, not MacDonald."[30] The primary legal issue centered on whether or not McGinniss had indeed led MacDonald to believe that he would present his life story positively. The lawsuit become the subject of *The Journalist and the Murderer*, Janet Malcolm's fascinating book, which first appeared as a two-part article in *The New Yorker.*

According to Malcolm, the MacDonald murder case initially appealed to McGinniss because he was allowed access to a subject—the preparation of a murder defense—that is typically privileged information. Malcolm maintains that "although none of us ever completely outgrows the voyeurism of childhood, in some of us it lives on more strongly than in others—thus the avid interest of some of us," McGinniss, for example, "in being 'insiders' or in getting the 'inside' view of things."[31] Malcolm's explanation identifies one of the central appeals of much literary journalism. Whether it is Gay Talese's *Thy Neighbor's Wife*, Tom Wolfe's *The Right Stuff*, or McGinniss' *Fatal Vision*, these and many other works of contemporary nonfiction provide glimpses into unfamiliar and often forbidden worlds that appeal to the voyeuristic interests of both journalists and readers. In some instances, this is realized not only by exploring unusual subject matter but also by probing the depths of human nature and confronting—in others and in ourselves—what lies beneath the surface of normal, everyday life. This has particular significance for writers of nonfiction—McGinniss, for example—who interpret the world and create characters out of their personal understanding of human experience. The subjects of a nonfiction work are based, of course, on real people, but they are also in part a symbolic creation of the author's inner, psychological world. Malcolm explains that they "derive from the writer's most idiosyncratic desires and deepest anxieties; they are what the writer wishes he was" or "worries that he is."[32] While it may indeed be an overstatement to suggest that in betraying and abandoning his wife and daughters for another woman McGinniss committed a symbolic murder comparable to his subject's very real and unimaginable acts, McGinniss' book does raise implicit questions about his and the reader's own capacity to commit murder while simultaneously mitigating our psychological complicity and guilt by presenting characters and situations—killing family members, for example—too awful for us to vicariously identify with, except perhaps on an unconscious level.

Like other writers of creative nonfiction, McGinniss may see parts of himself reflected in, or reveal himself in relation to, a symbolic other, but his emotional identification and friendship are superseded, at least in *Fatal Vision*, by a commitment to his writing: to dissolving personal attachments and creating a nonfiction character who ultimately represents, or coincides with, his understanding of human nature. Despite the fact that McGinniss and MacDonald are very similar (one of Malcolm's informants notes that they are both "traditional males . . . passionately interested in sports"[33] and another explains that "more than anything else in life" they both want to be liked[34]), Malcolm explains that McGinniss grew bored with MacDonald's self-serving monologue and ultimately "substitute[d] a story of his own."[35] Because MacDonald turned out to be an uninteresting character—"simply a guy like the rest of us"—McGinniss was forced to "fashion a Raskolnikov out of a Jeffrey MacDonald."[36] The solution to McGinniss' dilemma was achieved by transforming MacDonald into a psychopathic narcissist, an evil murderer. This allowed McGinniss to sever his emotional ties (friendship) with his subject and create a nonfiction character who would reflect his own understanding of human beings as fallible, even evil creatures. Malcolm explains that McGinniss' betrayal of MacDonald was an implicit but inescapable part of the author-subject agreement, for once writers begin writing their subjects invariably become characters in their own stories. "What gives journalism its authenticity and vitality is the tension between the subject's blind self-absorption and the journalist's skepticism. Journalists who swallow the subject's account whole and publish it are not journalists but publicists."[37]

Despite that McGinniss lost the lawsuit—he and his publisher settled out of court—in his following work of nonfiction, *Blind Faith*, he tells a similar, tragic tale about the death of another family member. On September 7, 1984, Maria Marshall, an attractive New Jersey homemaker and the mother of three boys—Chris, Rob, and John—was found shot to death in the front seat of her husband's Cadillac. The couple was returning home from an evening of dining and gambling in Atlantic City when Rob Marshall pulled into an unlighted and heavily wooded picnic area to check what he called a "mushy" tire. Husband Rob claimed that as he bent over the tire he had been struck on the head and when he regained consciousness he discovered his money gone and his wife dead. Not surprisingly, the Toms River police suspected that Marshall, a highly successful life insurance salesman and a prominent person in the community's business and social circles, was involved in the killing. The detectives investigating the murder discovered that Marshall was having an affair and planned to divorce his wife. He was also 300,000 dollars in debt and had insured Maria's life for 1.5 million dollars. Marshall was eventually convicted and sentenced to death for planning the murder of his wife and enlisting the help of a hired killer from Louisiana.

Of all of McGinniss' nonfiction, *Blind Faith* and *Fatal Vision* are the most conventional illustrations of factual reporting. Like the writing of Gay Talese and John McPhee, McGinniss seems principally interested in reconstructing these stories in specific and exacting detail. In fact, the thoroughness of his reporting not only establishes journalistic authority but implicitly introduces an epistemological framework, based on the authority of factual evidence, which gives rational coherence and meaning to a reality seemingly fraught with contradictions and uncertainty, absurdity and death. McGinniss' measured detachment and authorial aplomb—so different from the journalistic self presented in *Heroes*—introduces an element of literary control that gives symbolic order to a world gone temporarily haywire. More specifically, McGinniss' works are cultural morality tales focusing on the ambition, self-centeredness, and status-consciousness of two nominally ideal and successful Americans.

On the surface, MacDonald and Marshall appear to be two citizens who have identified—in their desire to succeed and achieve social distinction—with certain normative ideals dominant in our culture. As I suggest above, MacDonald's life reads, according to McGinniss, like the prototype of the American success story. MacDonald "escapes" his working-class background by winning a scholarship to Princeton and marrying his attractive, socially superior high-school girlfriend. Then there is medical school and children, followed by a distinguished internship at the prestigious Columbia Presbyterian Hospital. Though not as intelligent as MacDonald, Robert Marshall exhibits a similar ambition. Marshall's father (like McGinniss') was an alcoholic. Because he could not hold a job, the family was forced to move from one town to another. Rob's singular desire was to escape this debilitating and itinerant family life in order that he could make a success of himself. He spent a year in the Naval Reserves before he enrolled at Villanova. After graduation, Marshall went to Pensacola for Navy fight training and also married Maria Puszynski, the daughter of a successful Philadelphia physician. In the following year, Marshall was assigned to the Naval Air Station in Lakehurst, New Jersey, where he later became a life insurance salesman. In his first year he sold more than two million dollars worth of insurance and was one of the company's top fifty salesmen (nationwide). With this success came social recognition as well as the accumulation of material possessions. The joke around Toms River was that because "Howard Marshall [Rob's dad] died without ever having owned a house," Rob grew up "wanting to own everything he saw."[38]

Like Tom Wolfe, McGinniss frequently uses symbolic detail to help create a setting for his story and to underscore Rob Marshall's preoccupation with money and status. Even small, seemingly insignificant items have symbolic significance in McGinniss' reimagined social world: "Maria had given him [Rob] a combination pen and flashlight to make it easier for him to write in bed at night. Like many of the other possessions he'd acquired, it seemed to please him mostly because nobody else in Toms River had one."[39] McGinniss is particularly critical of Marshall, but it is clear, too, that his greed and acquisitiveness are emblematic of the entire Toms River country club set. While a court may have found Marshall guilty of murder, McGinniss indicts him and other Toms River residents for their moral and spiritual bankruptcy.

Marshall's preoccupation with status and material possessions is even the foundation of his relationship with his sons. The father affirms his position and power within the family by buying the love and devotion of his children with expensive status objects. While Rob drives an ivory Cadillac, he buys Roby a yellow Mustang, a Jeep for Chris, and the thirteen-year-old John is promised a Porsche—used, of course. Like the father, the sons are staunch supporters of this acquisitive lifestyle. In *Blind Faith*, as well as in *Fatal Vision*, the failure and shortcomings of the children are implicitly explained by the failure of the father as symbolic leader and by the crisis in the transfer of power from one generation to the next. This is true, for one, in Rob Marshall's relationship with his father: the itinerant life of an alcoholic father fostered a resentment in the son that resulted in the rejection of the parental figurehead and a repudiation of his past. Moreover, when the two oldest Marshall children come to believe their father Rob guilty of this heinous crime—the murder of their mother—they realize that their ideal life—material comforts and social status—no longer exists and perhaps never did. Only after the sons reject their father and acknowledge his guilt can they rid themselves of a destructively influential parental figure and create a life free of his influence. While the very real and figurative rejection of the father in *Blind Faith* may or may not be an unconscious and symbolic articulation of McGinniss' troubled relationship with his own father, it reveals, if nothing else, his preoccupation with flawed figures of authority who ultimately deviate from the normative ideal.

If Robert Marshall's character is in part explained by the absent father, Dr. Jeffrey MacDonald's nature is the product of an overbearing and charismatic father. In one of the many chapters in *Fatal Vision* titled "The Voice of Jeffrey MacDonald," McGinniss allows the former Green Beret and convicted murderer to tell his own story. MacDonald describes his father as "the leader and ruler" of the family. "His presence—it's almost beyond comprehension how important he was to the family." MacDonald goes on to explain that his father was "a very magnetic person . . . [with] a lot of charm and grace . . . [and] his hold on the family, even to this day, is staggering."[40] While MacDonald speaks of his father with the reverence of a dutiful son, he also notes that his father had an explosive temper, seldom expressed love or affection, and most important, demanded "absolute obedience" and achievement from his sons. MacDonald explains that "any indication that you couldn't keep up or couldn't be superior in every field—or try harder and overcome whatever adversity it was—was a sign of weakness."[41] MacDonald's relationship with his father is freighted with ambiguity: the aspiration and hard work of the all-American boy—college, medical school, the Army—are clearly attempts to fulfill the unrealistic expectations of a domineering father who can, in reality, never be appeased; no matter how much the son succeeds, he can only be a failure, for he can never fully live up to the grandiose image of the father that he has internalized and in part created.

MacDonald's failure as son/parent is realized in his own family life. MacDonald plays the role of ideal father/husband who shows his commitment to his family by being a successful provider. In fact, however, the many hours he spends away from home constitute a rejection of the family that he repeatedly—and somewhat suspiciously—claims is so wonderful, but that, in fact, only impedes his self-interests and commitment to success. The death of his family liberates him from the socially sanctioned bonds of marriage and the responsibility of raising children, while it allows him to pursue career goals unencumbered from the subconscious guilt of being an inadequate father/son.

At a time when the American family is in a state of crisis (or evolution), McGinniss suggests in *Fatal Vision* and *Blind Faith* that its most dominant threat comes from within the family itself. While McGinniss identifies this crisis in the lives of real and symbolic father figures, MacDonald and Marshall, the reader concludes, are not fully responsible for their crimes because they are by-products of a culture that encourages aggressive individualism and acquisitiveness as indices of success and fosters, as well, a destructive self-centeredness in allegedly model male Americans. In the epilogue of *Blind Faith*, McGinniss talks to one of Robert Marshall's sons. Roby tells McGinniss that his life has been totally transformed: " 'I have a life again,' " he explains. " 'And it's a life with a completely different set of values. I don't look at a lack of money as being a flaw anymore.' "[42] Roby is even dating a young woman from a working-class background—a woman he would not have considered before. While McGinniss is not overly heavy-handed, it is clear that Roby's statement, coming near the end of the book, is the lesson of this morality tale. The values and beliefs often associated with American life—aggressive individualism, acquisitiveness, among them—are, in extreme forms, the very vices that can corrupt and undermine the social order. In this respect, the stories told in *Fatal Vision* and *Blind Faith* are symbolic of a deeply rooted cultural ideology. More specifically, the excesses of Robert Marshall and Jeffrey MacDonald are particularly meaningful, even emblematic, in a decade, the

1980s, in which some cultural critics felt the venality and greed of young upwardly mobile Americans got out of control. In *Blind Faith*, as well as in a film like Oliver Stone's *Wall Street* (1987), commitment to meaningful human relationships, associated with the moral and ethical superiority of the working class, is clearly preferable to a life based on pecuniary gains, status consciousness, and material possessions. In *Fatal Vision* and *Blind Faith* McGinniss questions, as he does in all his works, the roles played by powerful figures in our culture and introduces traditional modes of analysis, the authority of storytelling, to make comprehensible a world in which some of our ideal and symbolic leaders—in these instances, fathers—have failed and betrayed us.

4

The Cultural Gamesmanship of Tom Wolfe

Thomas Kennerly Wolfe, Jr. was born and raised in Richmond, Virginia. Though his younger years were normal, even happy ones, Wolfe emphasizes that the "main thing about childhood was to get out of it. A child is at a great disadvantage. It's smaller than everyone else."[1] When Wolfe was nine, he began writing a biography of Napoleon. He explains that Napoleon "was small, and I was small. . . . It bothered me that the world was run by large people, and Napoleon was this little guy who, at one point, ran the world."[2] For a person who was acutely aware of, perhaps even subtly traumatized by, the lack of power he had as a child, it is not surprising that an older Tom Wolfe more readily privileges an omniscient authorial self and attends to the nuances of status and power in the construction of his carefully controlled social and literary worlds. Despite or perhaps because of this lack of power, Wolfe was a successful student and athlete. He attended public school through seventh grade and then enrolled at St. Christopher's, an Episcopal prep school for boys in Richmond. Wolfe made good grades; he enjoyed getting, he explains—perhaps with a hint of irony—"that extra smile from the teacher."[3] According to Toby Thompson, Wolfe "was a sensitive boy who studied tap and ballet, and who became an overachiever. He was an honors student, chairman of the student council, a fair athlete, and co-editor of the school newspaper."[4]

Wolfe attended Washington and Lee University—a private school in Lexington, Virginia—and graduated cum laude in 1951 with a bachelor's degree in English. He tried, unsuccessfully, to make the New York Giants as a professional pitcher. Wolfe then enrolled in the American Studies program at Yale University. After graduating with a Ph.D. in 1957, Wolfe turned down a job teaching history at a Midwest school. Though Wolfe indicated that he had had enough of academic life, his writings, as we shall see, are replete with scholarly references and certainly are more academic than the works of John McPhee, Joe McGinniss, and other literary journalists.

For a time, Wolfe worked as a furniture mover for a New Haven trucking firm. He quit after two months, however, and explained, years later, that there "is *no* insight to be gathered from the life of the working-class milieu."[5] Though as a journalist Wolfe has repeatedly emphasized the importance of "saturation reporting," the only personal insight gleaned from his blue-collar experience was a desire to escape from it. Wolfe may have repudiated the working-class life, but he still had an intellectual interest in how members of the proletariat and underground culture lived. He would come into New York, a friend explained, and "check into a welfare hotel on West 103rd street." Then the two of them would visit the "dives" in Greenwich Village. Wolfe "was very interested in Bohemia then," Wolfe's friend continues, "and he liked engaging these people in talks. But he didn't look like he *belonged* there."[6] Though Wolfe would later lampoon the Bernsteins and other liberals for their fashionable "slumming"—mixing with the Black Panther Party and other minority groups—his forays into Greenwich Village constitute a similar kind of *nostalgie de la boue* (nostalgia for the mud) and reveal, as we shall see, an outsider's inability to understand his subjects on their own economic, political, and ideological terms.

Following his brief employment as a furniture mover, Wolfe applied to more than one hundred newspapers. The Springfield *Union* was the only paper interested in hiring Wolfe. He worked for $55 a week and reported on town and sewer committee meetings.[7] In 1959 he was hired as a reporter and Latin American correspondent for the *Washington Post*. In 1962, three years before McPhee was hired by *The New Yorker*, Wolfe began writing for the *New York Herald Tribune* and contributing New Journalism pieces to the experimental Sunday section, *New York*, edited by Clay Felker. It was in writing a celebrated article for *Esquire*—"The Kandy-Kolored Tangerine-Flake Streamline Baby"—that Wolfe underwent a literary conversion experience and fully adopted a signature prose style that characterizes such later works as *The Electric Kool-Aid Acid Test* and *The Right Stuff*.

Wolfe's coverage of the California custom car world, the subject of the aforementioned article, also revealed an intensely personal interest in the exploration of subject matter—status groups and status group membership—which would later become the cornerstone of his literary nonfiction. In an interview with Joe David Bellamy, Wolfe was asked whether "the subject of status" was his "main territory or interest." He explained that it is "really more of an analytical tool than a subject per se. It's just so fundamental to everything that people do that it's going to come up. That's the first thing I always look for."[8] In fact, whereas John McPhee and Joe McGinniss focus on the lives of individuals, Wolfe asserts that the "fundamental unit in analyzing behavior is not the individual, but some sort of status group or status structure. Who is in competition with whom else and why? What are the stakes and rules?"[9] Wolfe's interest in status groups, status competition, and the implied rules governing social interaction all suggest that Wolfe's version of reality might best be understood when examined through the paradigm of the game metaphor.

While other literary journalists such as Hunter S. Thompson and Norman Mailer often participate in the events they later write about, Wolfe is rarely involved in the events he reports on and is never the central focus of his journalism stories. He is, nonetheless, the quintessential and master gamesman whose presence is strongly felt despite his conspicuous absence. This is, of course, in part a presence of language, of style, as Chris Anderson explains in *Style as Argument: Contemporary American Nonfiction*,[10] but it is also a more fundamental and symbolic positioning of self. As readers, we know Wolfe for his style of dress, as the flamboyant and foppishly attired social critic who bemusedly comments on the follies and foibles of others. When asked once if he owned a pair of jeans, Wolfe acknowledged that he did—one pair—but he never wore them below the third floor. Though Wolfe's response is intended to be humorous, his presentation of self is more than stylish posturing and paying deference to high fashion. Wolfe reveals, for example, that when he lived in Richmond, " 'no respectable man went out in casual clothes. They just don't feel right to me.' "[11] He explains that his father " 'always had his clothes made in Richmond. It was not considered a big deal. I started having mine made in Washington. Unlike him, I became very conscious of it.' "[12] " 'Never underestimate,' " Wolfe adds, " 'how much of your childhood is sewn into the lining of your garments when you go to New York.' "[13] Even when doing work at home, Wolfe wears either a jacket and tie or a suit—more often a suit. Clothes are clearly, as the following passage suggests, a fundamental part of who Wolfe is and reveal, as well, the part of himself he is willing to make public: "every person's 'real self,' his psyche, his soul, is largely the product of fashion and other outside influences on his status."[14]

While Wolfe does call attention to himself with his clothes, they also provide a barrier—a cloak of invisibility—that keeps others, Wolfe's friend observed, " 'from focusing on more personal things.' "[15] Wolfe admits to being a very private person; he explains that in Richmond people were more stoic and did not discuss personal anxieties and problems (as people do in New York).[16] He believes that repression can often be of positive value. " 'Negative emotions feed on each other' " he explains, so " 'it's probably better to let some of them remain nameless.' "[17] Wolfe's Southern heritage may in part explain his personal and journalistic reticence, but it just as likely reveals, I believe, a characteristic unwillingness of a number of male literary journalists to fully explore the psychological and emotional relationship between self and other, or journalist and subject. Wolfe appears to believe in the inviolability of the private self, but it is unclear whether he consciously respects the personal lives of his subjects or is unable as a journalist, assuming a role of cool detachment, to probe the interior life of the people about whom he writes. While a literary journalist such as Gay Talese may frequently reveal what his subjects are thinking and feeling, Wolfe almost uniformly focuses on their public behavior and social identity. Wolfe's work may not be intensely autobiographical, nor does he share the same values and beliefs with his subjects as John McPhee does with his; the manner in which he presents himself to the world, however, is reflected in what he finds significant in his examination of others.

More specifically, Wolfe's style of dress and presentation of self have rhetorical and symbolic as well as sociological significance, as they do in the writings of Hunter S. Thompson. In the opening pages of *The Electric Kool-Aid Acid Test*, for example, Wolfe the social actor appears, rather uncharacteristically, at the beginning of the Pranksters' story. He is riding in the back of a truck with several of the Pranksters. One of them, Black Maria, asks:

> "When is your birthday?"
> "March 2."
> "Pisces," she says, And then: "I would never take you for a Pisces."
> "Why?"
> "You seem too . . . *solid* for a Pisces."[18]

Wolfe tells the reader that "I know she meant stolid. I am beginning to feel stolid. Back in New York City, Black Maria, I tell you, I am even known as something of a dude. But somehow a blue silk blazer and a big tie with a clown on it and . . . a . . . pair of shiny lowcut black shoes don't set them all doing the Varsity Rag in the head world in San Francisco."[19] Several pages later, while all the Pranksters parade around the "Warehouse" in a variety of colorful costumes, Wolfe reminds the reader that he is faithfully attired in his three-piece suit. Wolfe the author does not intend to define his journalistic self as a character in the work, nor does he establish himself as a witness to authenticate his story as, for example, John McPhee and other literary journalists do. Wolfe maintains, in fact, that standing out as a journalist, as he portrays himself in the opening pages of this book, works to his advantage in gathering information. "People really don't want you to try to fit in," Wolfe explains. "They'd much rather fill you in. People like to have someone to tell their stories to. So if you're willing to be the village information gatherer, they'll often just pile material on you."[20] While Wolfe suggests that his clothes encourage subjects to provide information they might not ordinarily disclose, his trademark three-piece suit also identifies his affinity with satirist Mark Twain and constitutes, in the author's own words, "a harmless form of aggression."[21] In addition, Wolfe's signature attire represents a unique metaphor of self—a statement of personal and perhaps class identity—that affirms the cultural space that separates him from his subjects; it identifies Wolfe as a mainstream journalist whose ostensible role is to describe and unmask this and other alien subcultures for a group of educated, middle-class readers.

The examination of arcane worlds and societies is certainly one of the basic appeals of New Journalism, but it is a fundamental part of Wolfe's work. Wolfe's journalistic occasions are comparable to the efforts made by ethnographers to document, if not salvage, primitive and vanishing cultures. Wolfe makes overtures to explain subcultures on their own terms, but in reality he describes and understands them all with a strikingly similar method and a language that is distinctly his own. In fact, Wolfe's richly textured verbal performance encourages readers to attend to the surface of language and recognize that a self—at least the presence of an authorial self—is declared in the articulation of a distinct literary style. While McPhee's restrained and "realistic" writing may nominally cloak the authorial self, Wolfe's literary pyrotechnics underscore his presence on most every page. Wolfe's scrupulous attention to the surface of American life—notably, the dress and hairstyles of his subjects—is matched and complemented by his highly visible linguistic performance and style.

As master gamesman, Wolfe also establishes a privileged position based on the power relation between the powerful observer and the less powerful observed. This is determined principally by the management of information. Whereas John McPhee proposes a democratic epistemology based on a distribution of information that is public and shared, Wolfe more selectively controls the flow of information and lets readers believe that they are privy to esoteric knowledge that is withheld from (or unknown to) others. In describing the interaction of social players, for example, Wolfe is able to discern a truth about characters that they themselves cannot understand but that he can astutely observe and document. Wolfe is, finally, the master gamesman whose journalistic performance is predicated upon his ability to establish the rules of the game and lead the reader to believe that they (the rules) are actually part of the reality they signify.

In *The Electric Kool-Aid Acid Test*, for example, Wolfe suggests that there is a game-like interaction between the Merry Pranksters and certain members of mainstream culture. Kesey's and the Pranksters' interaction with the police is identified as the "cops-and-robbers" game. The Pranksters themselves, Ken Kesey in particular, are aware that their identities are determined by socially prescribed or proscribed roles. Their acquired appellations—Neal Cassady is known as "Speed Limit," for example, and Kesey is "Chief"—are ironically chosen to illustrate how one's individuality is subsumed by a name that is determined either by a social role or a single, usually superficial, trait. In "Mau-Mauing the Flak Catchers" Wolfe maintains that white civil servants "sat back and waited for you to come rolling in with your certified angry militants, your frustrated ghetto youth." Then the flak catchers (civil servants) knew—"if you were outrageous enough, if you could shake up the bureaucrats so bad"—which groups deserved the community organizing jobs and poverty grants.[22] In both these works, Wolfe uses a method for interpreting social phenomena, the game metaphor, that is congruent with his subjects' understanding of their own experiences. Wolfe implies that the behavior of social actors is informed by a goal-directedness when he interprets their interaction as a dramatized (or staged) confrontation; the social players, civil servants and "certified angry militants," knew the "rules" of the game, acted accordingly, and anticipated the expected rewards at the conclusion of the encounter. Ethnic and minority groups received poverty grants, while civil servants were assured that they had made the right choice in distributing those grants. While a number of cultural critics and historians interpreted the interaction between mainstream culture and various adversarial groups in more "serious" terms—as a symbolic and often real clash of value structures—Wolfe astutely recognized the calculated, even playful interaction between groups whose members presumably understood the tacit, if not overt, rules of the social game.

Generally, however, Wolfe is less successful in explaining in "Mau-Mauing the Flak Catchers" and other works how social players come to understand the rules governing their behavior. While a minority leader named Chaser seems to be cognizant of the "game" he is playing—"he had everything planned out on his side, right down to the last detail,"[23] Wolfe tells us—he is more equivocal when he remarks that there were residents living in the Western Addition "who practically gave classes in Mau-Mauing."[24] While the usefulness of the game model does not depend on awareness in the social actors, Wolfe himself is at times unsure of how the game and its rules originated. He often relies on a teleological interpretation of social interaction: "The strange thing was that the confrontation ritual was built into the poverty program from the beginning," Wolfe maintains. "The poverty bureaucrats" relied on these confrontations to determine what to do.[25] But how did the poverty bureaucrats *know* that they had to depend on the confrontations to know what to do? While Wolfe suggests that his interpretation of culture is based on the observation of, and the interaction between, social players, the frame of sociological analysis is mistakenly employed to explain, I believe, the ostensible goal-directedness of the principal actors. Wolfe discerns a pattern in a number of social situations and then proposes that it was consciously conceived by the social players. This allows Wolfe to disguise his method of social analysis by suggesting that it is an inherent part of the subject and a prerequisite for making sense of it.

Wolfe's authority as journalist and social critic is founded, in fact, chiefly on his ability to reveal what others—press members or social players—are not able to recognize or articulate. In *The Right Stuff*, for instance, Wolfe says, in discussing "the right stuff," that "none of this was to be mentioned, and yet it was acted out in a way that a young man could not fail to understand."[26] In another example, Wolfe asks why members of the press, and seemingly every other human being, were so emotionally moved that they created instant heroes of the seven Mercury astronauts. He explains that "this was a question that not James Reston or the pilots themselves or anyone of NASA could have answered at the time, because the very language of the proposition had long since been abandoned and forgotten. The forgotten term, left behind in the superstitious past, was *single combat*."[27] *The Right Stuff* is filled with similar comments: "The message seemed to be"[28]; "No one spoke the phrase"[29]; "No one knew its name"[30]; and "that was probably unconscious on Al's part."[31] In "Radical Chic," to draw from another work, Don Cox, field marshal of the Black Panther Party, talks to the group of socialites and Panthers who have gathered at Leonard and Felicia Bernstein's penthouse duplex in support of the twenty-one Black Panthers who had been arrested on charges of conspiring to blow up five New York department stores. Wolfe says this about his speech: "But everyone here loves the *sees* and the *you knows*. They are so, somehow . . . *black* . . . so *funky* . . . so metrical. . . . Without ever bringing it fully into consciousness everyone responds—communes over—the fact that he uses them not for emphasis but for punctuation."[32] While many of Wolfe's characters, particularly in *The Right Stuff*, act without being cognizant of what governs their behavior, Wolfe, who is able to articulate the unnameable ("single combat") and make the "unconscious" recognizable or transparent, penetrates the insular and reticent world of the fighter jock and claims, implicitly at least, to discern what others cannot. He establishes himself as the only player—and usually omniscient narrator—who has full knowledge of the game.

This helps establish, of course, Wolfe's authority as a cultural critic. In addition, it implicitly suggests that it is in part the superior form of communication, the New Journalism, that allows him to understand and explain what other press members cannot. Like many other literary journalists—most notably Hunter S. Thompson and Norman Mailer—Wolfe criticizes mainstream journalists for their inability to act autonomously. In *The Right Stuff* he repeatedly refers to the press as either "the Genteel Beast" or "the Victorian Gent"—a great colonial animal . . . made up of countless clustered organisms responding to a single nervous system." Wolfe explains that "the animal seemed determined that in all matters of national importance the *proper emotion*, the *seemly sentiment*, the *fitting moral tone* should be established and should prevail."[33] Though Wolfe does not fully explain what conditions foster this phenomenon, commonly known as "pack" or "herd" journalism, he criticizes reporters for a behavioral and institutional conformity in which they allegedly have no control over while he articulates an imperial journalistic self that defies, or escapes from, the tyrannizing rules governing nearly all social membership.

While it is common for many New Journalists to rely on first-hand experience, gathering material from witnessed events, Wolfe's two most successful works, *The Electric Kool-Aid Acid Test* and *The Right Stuff*, are based largely on information gathered from secondary sources: interviews, public documents, letters, and so on. In part, I believe, Wolfe relies greatly on secondary sources because he is unwilling to participate in events or become too intimate with subjects about whom he later writes; he refuses to relinquish personal control by stepping out of his role as detached observer/cultural critic and confronting—as Hunter S. Thompson and Norman Mailer do—the "raw" experience of life. Like John McPhee, Wolfe seems to feel more comfortable as a journalist and person when he can orchestrate the dynamics of social encounters and tacitly claim an implied power associated with his allegedly neutral journalistic perspective.

The success of Wolfe's journalistic and interpretive performance is largely based on his scholarly training, on his ability to wed historical and esoteric ideas and insights to contemporary incidents and ordinary events. In *The Electric Kool-Aid Acid Test*, for example, Wolfe illuminates the religious dimension of The Merry Pranksters' experience by comparing it to other historical religious movements: Christianity, Buddhism, Judaism, and so on. Similarly, in "Radical Chic" Wolfe interprets the courting of Black Panthers by wealthy New York liberals as a recent manifestation of the historically established practice of "slumming": cultivating "low-rent" styles and mixing with people of a lower social class. While Wolfe tries to demystify alien cultural experiences and make them intelligible to his readers, he relies on conventional and historically established information and frames of reference derived from mainstream culture. Wolfe establishes journalistic authority by defining his role as a cultural interpreter—a disembodied voice—who gives historical depth to events that are ostensibly peculiar to the moment—at some expense, of course. As David Eason points out, Wolfe yokes all idiosyncratic views of reality to "a well-ordered, non-threatening past that promises to extend into the future."[34] In this respect, Wolfe minimizes—and at times depoliticizes—contemporary experience by encoding it in familiar terms and past social contexts.

Within a specific text (and context)—for instance, "Radical Chic"—Wolfe tries to position himself as an objective observer who is ostensibly interested in chronicling the political dialogue between two disparate social groups, Black Panthers and New York liberals. Wolfe often describes this and other social moments from not one or two, but three points of view: his own perspective, his subject's, and that of other spectators. He uses "substitutionary narration," moreover, to imitate and even parody his subjects in order to understand and represent them from the perspective of outsiders or onlookers.[35] In the following passage, for example, Wolfe assumes the voice/perspective of California surfers, members of the Pump House gang, and pokes fun at a pair of middle-aged tourists:

> All of these kids, seventeen of them . . . are lollygagging around the stairs down to Windansea Beach, La Jolla, California, about 11 A.M., and they all look at the black feet, which are a woman's pair of black street shoes, out of which stick a pair of old veiny white ankles, which lead up like a senile cone to a fudge of tallowy, edematous flesh, her thighs, squeezing out of her bathing suit, with old faded yellow bruises on them, which she probably got from running eight feet to

catch a bus or something. She is standing with her old work-a-hubby, who has on *sandals*: you know, a pair of navy-blue anklet socks and these sandals with big, wide, new-smelling tan straps going this way and that, *for keeps*. Man, they look like orthopedic sandals, if one can imagine that. Obviously these people come from Tucson or Albuquerque or one of those hincty adobe towns.[36]

While Wolfe attempts to represent the perspectives of his subjects in these two works, more often than not, all discordant voices are subverted, or superseded, by the monophonic and ideological authority of the transcendent observer. While Wolfe's writing nominally represents a democratic mode of expression, it implicitly reveals, as does most literary journalism, both a tacit literary and social elitism and a traditional and conservative interpretation of contemporary American experience. According to David Eason, the "ethnographic realism" of Wolfe and other literary journalists "constitutes the subculture as an object of display, and the reporter and reader, whose values are assumed and not explored, are cojoined in the act of observing." Eason adds that the "effect of this strategy is to reinvent textually the consensus which cultural fragmentation had called into question."[37] Wolfe naturalizes discrepant realities by suggesting that the method used is the most commonsensical way, if not the only way, of making sense of such contemporary experiences. Though Wolfe criticizes other conventional journalists for their institutional allegiances, his journalism authority and method of cultural analysis arise from his scholarly training at Yale, from his class position within a hierarchical institutional and academic order.

The social game is thematically and formally understood, as I noted, on personal and ideologically conservative terms. Wolfe's exploration of subcultural experience, for example, might be superficially interpreted as a celebration of cultural diversity and American pluralism. Wolfe explains that the proliferation of subcultures and status systems was due primarily to the post–World War II economic boom. Behind the cataloguing of exotic status symbols is, in other words, an underlying economic interpretation of subcultural experience that links it to the ideological and material superstructure of mainstream culture. Wolfe refuses to acknowledge, however, that the emergence of a succession of youth cultures and subcultural styles might constitute a form of symbolic opposition that reveals a more general dissatisfaction with American life. Instead, Wolfe minimizes ideological and political dissent by focusing on style and interpreting conflict in rhetorical and literary terms.

In part, Wolfe achieves dramatic tension by bifurcating the world into a rigid we-they polarity. In *The Electric Kool-Aid Acid Test*, for example,

Wolfe notes "that the world is sheerly divided into those who have had *the experience* and those who have not—those who have been through the door—" (that is, taken LSD).[38] Throughout *The Right Stuff* we are reminded that there are those who have it—"the right stuff"—and there are those who do not. Wolfe expresses, of course, the collective feelings shared by members of each status group, the Merry Pranksters and test pilots, and successfully dramatizes and exposes status competition, both between and within status structures. In *The Right Stuff* there is, to name a few, the rivalry between fighter pilots and astronauts, astronauts and engineers, and the astronauts themselves. Overshadowing these conflicts is the race between the United States and the Soviet Union to control the heavens. Though the race to conquer space had a political and ideological base, Wolfe's journalistic treatment is principally literary and polemical; he is most interested in the drama, tension, and hysteria behind the space flights and the disparity between Soviet successes and U.S. failures. The race into space is reduced almost to an Olympic competition between countries with a familiar protagonist hero (the United States) vying against an equally familiar, evil antagonist (Russia).

As compelling as Wolfe's writing is in this case, he often overly emphasizes status competition and competitive social interaction and inadequately accounts for the cooperation that occurs between social players. In "Radical Chic," for example, Wolfe is so intent on exposing status incongruities that he does not acknowledge that the "radical chic" evening might be conceived as a bona fide attempt, however superficial and ineffectual, to meliorate social differences and promote racial harmony. Wolfe's insistent preoccupation with status and status differences, in fact, might be interpreted as perverting, or at least undermining, the implied rules of this and other social games. The game can only be played if participants play by the rules of the specific encounter or gathering. Theoretically speaking, power, status, wealth, beauty, strength, knowledge—all relevant in many other social contexts—are extrinsic to (this) specific game interactions.[39] Wolfe's devotion to status detail, in other words, is somewhat, if not entirely, irrelevant to how these social players—Bernstein (and friends) and the Black Panthers—participate in this particular encounter. In order for the game to succeed, it is necessary that members from both status groups minimize their social differences and recognize that they both can benefit, as social antagonists allegedly do in "Mau-Mauing the Flak Catchers," by abiding by the acknowledged and tacit rules of the social interaction.

Wolfe would have us believe, however, that cooperation between status groups is almost impossible. In both *The Painted Word* and *From Bauhaus to Our House*, Wolfe repeatedly indicates that the artist (painter and architect) is tyrannized by the desire to separate himself from the "hated" middle-class—"to cut himself forever free from the bonds of the greedy and hypocritical bourgeoisie."[40] Similarly, Wolfe maintains that "composers, artists, or architects in a compound began to have the instincts of the medieval clergy, much of whose activity was devoted exclusively to separating itself from the mob. For mob, substitute bourgeoisie."[41] While Wolfe clearly reveals that status competition figures more prominently in the world of art than people believe, he frames this discussion in the form of an argument replete with egregious historical and analytical reductionism and identifies a personal metaphor of self—a preoccupation with status and class—by implicitly revealing a symbolic and perhaps real desire to separate himself as an artist (New Journalist) and person from the "hated" bourgeoisie (conventional journalists). Though status competition explains much, it cannot begin to explain why an artist, let alone a great number of artists, produces a particular work of art. The homogenizing nature of consensus history (and social criticism) provides a tidy and reassuring picture of how the world works and helps certify the conceptual and explanatory powers of the author. Generalizations and encompassing statements—"every artist knew," for example, and "every soul here"[42]—underscore Wolfe's facile ability to sum up a particular world and make it intelligible. In "Radical Chic" Wolfe punctuates the narrative with his use of "everyone," as in "everyone in here loves the *sees* and the. . . . "[43] A claimed consensus and Wolfe's implied omniscience—the ability to know what others are thinking and feeling—buttress his authority and objectify his personal interpretations. This is one way in which Wolfe implicates readers and benignly coerces them into seeing the world on his personal and metaphorical terms.

Wolfe's writing, like all written works, addresses a particular audience and establishes communication between a specific sender (author) and a more general receiver (reader). While Wolfe's manner of address may be more indirect than, for example, Joan Didion's, he establishes, nonetheless, an implicit pact in which the reader is privy to the author's knowledge and superior insights. Just as Wolfe divides the world into us-them polarities, so Wolfe and his readers share insights and knowledge about the social and artistic worlds unknown to others. While this interaction of writer and reader is often dialogic, predicated in part upon an open-end text, Wolfe, in fact, establishes a closed interpretive frame and defines the reader as a cooperating participant in the communication exchange. This entente among insiders is established in part by disclosing privileged information to the reader, but also by the manner of Wolfe's rhetorical address. In "Radical Chic," for example, Wolfe's repeated use of "deny it if you want to" (or "deny it if you wish to") challenges and implicates the reader and, finally, dictates only one response: "But, of course," the reader is supposed to say. "That is how it really is." Richard A. Kallan explains, moreover, that Wolfe's writing is "packaged without qualification. It is not 'I think,' 'It would appear,' 'One might conclude.' Nor do qualifiers such as 'sometimes,' 'usually,' or 'perhaps' preface any of Wolfe's statements. The style connotes assuredness and promotes the sensation that everything described is obvious and absolute."[44]

In describing and distinguishing one "statusphere" from another, Wolfe generally relies on careful observation and documentation of symbolic details—clothes, speech, hairstyle. On one "radical chic" occasion, for example, Wolfe observes that "the grape workers were all in work clothes, Levi's, chinos, Sears balloon-seat twills, K-Mart sports shirts, and so forth. The socialites, meanwhile, arrived at the height of the 1969 summer season of bell-bottom silk pants suits, Pucci clings, Dunhill blazers, and Turnbull & Asser neckerchiefs."[45] Because Wolfe focuses so relentlessly on status minutiae, the personal and psychological dimensions of his subjects are often ignored, or are addressed only by implication. For example, while Wolfe nominally portrays the test pilots in *The Right Stuff* as individuals, we are given only a few superficial details of each person and one general characteristic to define them all: that is, of course, "the right stuff." Wolfe suggests that association with a status group is the primary way in which identity is determined. The personal (or core self) is usurped by a socially constructed public identity based on status group membership. By not probing beneath the surface of his subjects, Wolfe reaffirms his belief in the sanctity of a private self and suggests that emotions and personal idiosyncrasies are of little consequence in understanding or illuminating human nature. Morris Dickstein maintains that Wolfe's subjects are merely "manikins of chic, butts of social satire"; that even when he writes from inside his characters "their subjective reality remains stubbornly uninteresting." Wolfe ultimately homogenizes "his characters into one inner voice . . . a collective embodiment of a social attitude."[46] In other words, according to Dickstein, Wolfe is more interested in portraying a static idea—a status distinction, conflict, or incongruity—than with dramatizing diverse interactions of psychologically individuated selves.

Wolfe, of course, often relies on caricature, and he is as capable as any social critic at characterizing and satirizing types. There is the garrulous and cloyingly friendly Texan in *The Right Stuff*, referred to as Herb Snout: " 'Hi, there little Lady! Just *damned* glad to see *you*, too!' And then he'd give a huge horrible wink that would practically implode his eye, and he'd say, 'We've heard a lot of good things about you gals, a *lot* of good things'—all with that eye-wrenching wink."[47] In *The Electric Kool-Aid Acid Test* and *The Right Stuff*, doctors (and scientists), referred to as white smocks, are summarily portrayed as impersonal and unfriendly. In *The Right Stuff*, this depiction of doctors allegedly illustrates the typical test pilot or astronaut's feelings about members from this status group. While Wolfe successfully uses stereotypes and caricature to convey animosity between these status structures, his satirical portraits can be unflattering, narrow, snobbishly prejudiced, to some even sexist, racist, and brutal. In "*A* Wolfe *in* Chic Clothing," Christopher Hitchens questions Wolfe's frequent use of racial and minority stereotypes. In "Mau-Mauing the Flak Catchers," for example, Wolfe delineates Samoans in the following fashion:

> Everything about them is gigantic, even their heads. They'll have a skull the size of a watermelon, with a couple of little squinty eyes and a little mouth and a couple of nose holes stuck in, and no neck at all. From the ears down, the big yoyos are just one solid welded hulk, the size of an oil burner. . . . They have big wide faces and smooth features. They're a dark brown, with a smooth cast.[48]

Wolfe talks about Chinese, Mexicans, and blacks in a similar sophomoric manner. Hitchens comes to the conclusion that while Wolfe depends heavily on racial caricature, it is a "sign of laziness rather than prejudice."[49] In "Radical Chic," however, Hitchens maintains that "Wolfe is striking much harder than a [responsible] satirist would. His intention was really to do harm, and he succeeded brilliantly."[50]

Of all the status structures and groups Wolfe describes and satirizes, women are portrayed, more often than not, in the most unflattering terms. In "Radical Chic," for example, Wolfe makes at least three references to an allegedly naive but "beautiful ash-blond girl." On one occasion, Wolfe reports that she wants to know what she can personally do, without money or political power, to help the Black Panthers. "Well, baby, if you really"—Wolfe begins, then he goes on to quote Don Cox, who tells her that she could look for churches that would help sponsor the Panther's breakfast program for ghetto children.[51] Wolfe's initial comment—"Well, baby, if you really"—suggests, if nothing else, that she can donate her liberal body to the cause. Clearly, Wolfe is taking liberties by inventing and attributing thoughts to one of his characters, Don Cox, at the young woman's expense.

Throughout Wolfe's writing, women are described in a similar fashion. In *The Electric Kool-Aid Acid Test* he notes that the "West Coast" was "always full of . . . long-haired little Wasp and Jewish buds balling spade cats."[52] Wolfe may be suggesting, of course, that such coupling is merely a more intimate yet equally fashionable form of consorting with "raw-vital, Low Rent primitives." This and other comments raise questions, nonetheless, about Wolfe's depiction of women. At the Southern stock car races, Wolfe notes, you always see "these beautiful little buds in short shorts . . . spread-eagle out on the top of the car roofs, pressing down on good hard slick automobile sheet metal, their little cupcake bottoms aimed up at the sun."[53] Wolfe's writing may not be intentionally sexist, but his portrayal of women and his use of stereotypes and satire raise questions about his moral and social responsibility to his subjects, even if they figure only marginally into his work. Because Wolfe depicts women unsympathetically, he tacitly conspires with his main subjects—the astronauts, for example—in constructing a masculine world based in part on the exploitation of women. In a 1983 interview, Wolfe candidly admitted that the "gang bang" described in *The Electric Kool-Aid Acid Test* was a "horrible scene." Yet, Wolfe's almost comedic treatment of the event—he describes the woman as "some blond from out of town . . . just one nice soft honey hormone squash"[54]—points to his inability to deal sensitively with women's experiences. For a journalist who claims to be a chronicler of contemporary society, much like Balzac was in his day, it is somewhat surprising that Wolfe—and for that matter, other male literary journalists—ignored almost entirely two of the most important subjects of the 1960s and early 1970s, the "sexual revolution" and the women's movement.

Wolfe's depiction of women, his satirical portraits, as well as his stereotypes and status group generalizations, reveal the political affiliation and social class biases of an educated white male. His chosen journalistic role of detached observer and the use of omniscient narration, as well as subtitutionary narration, reflect the social space that separates him from, and perhaps elevates him above, many of his subjects. Wolfe's use of satire and his preoccupation with status details, furthermore, allow him to maintain unimpeded control of the re-imagined social game. If his characters were more dramatically rounded and more psychologically complex, they would acquire identities resistant to stereotyping, satiric snobbery, and status group identification. As it is, Wolfe's subjects possess no such voice or identity of their own; they remain participants in a game defined, played, and interpreted by the master gamesman in the white suit, Thomas Kennerly Wolfe, Jr.

5

The Minimal Self: Joan Didion's Journalism of Survival

Joan Didion was born a fifth-generation Californian, something of a rarity in our most populous state. The majority of her childhood and adolescence was spent in the Sacramento Valley. Throughout her younger years she was regularly reminded, particularly in Sunday school, that the valley was a sacred place, "a fertile Eden." Katherine Usher Henderson explains that the "Sacramento Valley is splendid in its natural beauty, but it was its provincial insulation from the outside world that contributed most strongly to the persistence of this Edenic myth."[1] Didion's idyllic world was temporarily disrupted during World War II, however, when her father, an Air Corpsman, was transferred four times (and to three different states) in only three years. When the family returned to Sacramento after the war, "it was a long time," according to Henderson, before Didion "regained the sense of belonging that she had felt as a small child."[2] Though Didion maintains that her childhood years were normal, she was, according to Michiko Kakutani, "a fearful child—scared of ski lifts, of rattlesnakes in the river, even of comic books, filled as they were with violence and monsters."[3] Didion was also bothered by recurrent disaster fantasies, and suicide was a consistent theme throughout her earliest (unpublished) short stories, written a couple of years after her return to Sacramento. While it is difficult to determine the influence of childhood preoccupations on the adult self, it is clearly evident that an older Didion continues to externalize private concerns and fears in very personal, metaphorical readings of the world. While this personal and psychological mark of identity persists throughout her writings, Didion's sense of self is also determined by geography and history. Her respect for the privacy of others and her belief in the sanctity of an imperial self come out of a "Western frontier ethic": "being left alone and leaving others alone," according to Didion, was considered by her family members "as the highest form of human endeavor."[4] Not surprisingly, then, though the symbolic family and home are of critical importance in Didion's work, particularly in *Slouching Towards Bethlehem*, rarely does she talk specifically about her own family life. This reticence, as Henderson points out, derives "in part from a respect for their privacy, but it certainly also derives from her conviction that we are molded less by our personal interaction with our parents than by our genes, our biochemistry, and our historical time and place."[5]

Though Didion may indeed respect the privacy of her subjects, her works of nonfiction—most notably, *Slouching Towards Bethlehem* and *The White Album*—are characterized by unremitting self-scrutiny, by a public declaration of her most intimate and private concerns. Throughout her work, Didion invokes and confronts moments from her past and, as Chris Anderson notes, "dramatizes herself in the act of telling a story that can have no ending."[6] Even when Didion identifies herself as a detached, disembodied social critic, she turns "cultural fact into a personal iconography which then becomes the medium of interpretation."[7] Alfred Kazin explains that many American writers—and this is true of Didion—"tend to project the world as a picture of themselves even when they are not writing directly about themselves."[8] This is most evident in Didion's metaphorical reading of the material world: disorder, accelerated change, random violence, and death, as she repeatedly underscores, seem to be the principal realities of human experience. This private projection onto a natural and socially constructed world is the constituent metaphor of her four works of nonfiction: *Slouching Towards Bethlehem*, *The White Album*, *Salvador*, and *Miami*. In an unstable and an unpredictable world—in which the only thing "constant about the California of" Didion's "childhood is the rate at which it disappears."[9]—writing about the self and its disjunctures becomes an increasingly meaningful but problematic activity. Didion's autobiographical occasions, particularly in *Slouching Towards Bethlehem*, are predicated on a seemingly irreconcilable dilemma: the need to affirm a personal and historical identity within a society that repudiates the past and promises no stable or recognizable future. While McPhee articulates a stable, inner-directed self embodied in the model of the authentic (ideal) American, Didion repeatedly acknowledges the difficulty of maintaining a central, coherent identity. Didion's belief in the nominal sovereignty of the imperial self is repeatedly challenged and in part shaped, as it is in the writings of Hunter S. Thompson, by factors outside her control. While Erik Erikson locates the identity crisis in the developmental period of adolescence and youth, Didion invites us to interpret her adult experiences as a series of personal identity crises. In addition, though Didion recognizes the importance of the examined self—"we are all well advised," she admonishes, "to keep on nodding terms with the people we used to be"[10]—she acknowledges a desire to reveal herself without fully declaring her individuality when she writes about places and other people. In her discussion of women's autobiography, Patricia Meyer Spacks explains that for some women "the identity of public performance may cause its female possessor"—and this seems to be true of Didion—"to experience intensely, or at any rate to reveal emphatically, pre-existent uncertainties of personal identity. Such uncertainties," she surmises, "take special form and receive special emphasis in women's accounts of their lives."[11] As we shall see, this seems to be reflected in Didion's need to occasionally "disappear," as a journalist and person, from the public worlds she occupies and describes.

Though Didion may indeed "disappear," or "hide" a self, she implicitly acknowledges, in James Olney's words, that "the subjective self must always be prior to a sense of the objective world."[12] In "On Keeping a Notebook," for example, Didion indicates that the reason she keeps a journal "has never been, nor is it now, to have an accurate factual record of what I have been doing or thinking."[13] At one time in her life, Didion tried "faithfully" to document a day's events but finally "abandoned altogether that kind of pointless entry." Instead, she adds, "I tell what some would call lies." When Didion and her family members are recalling an event experienced together, for example, her recollections are often challenged by a parent or a sibling: " 'That's simply not true,' " one of them says. Didion acknowledges that "very likely they are right, for not only have I always had trouble distinguishing between what happened and what merely might have happened, but I remain unconvinced that the distinction, for my purposes, matters."[14] Like Hunter S. Thompson, Didion identifies and re-invents, "telling episodes that present a life story [or events] more truthfully than what actually happened."[15] For Didion, the factual, objective reality of her past experiences is subordinate to both the transforming power of memory and the shaping conscious of the writer. Didion would firmly endorse Georges Gusdorf's conviction that autobiographical writing "is a second reading of experience, and it is truer than the first because it adds to experience itself consciousness of it."[16] While a literary journalist like McPhee hides a private self behind a constructed world nominally based on an objective reality, Didion candidly admits that her abiding commitment to journal writing—in fact, to all writing—allows her to "*remember what it was to be me.*"[17] Her commitment to a personal and at times private self takes precedent over commitment to the material world; the "common denominator" in all her work, Didion emphasizes, "is always, transparently, shamelessly, the implacable 'I.' "[18] When she explains that writing allows her "to keep on nodding terms with the people" she used to be,[19] she acknowledges both the provisional nature of identity formation and the therapeutic value of reintegrating former (past) selves with the adult Joan Didion.

Throughout *Slouching Towards Bethlehem*, for example, Didion reveals—on personal, cultural, and symbolic levels—an intense preoccupation with childhood and children. In "On Going Home" Didion returns to her childhood home in Sacramento, California accompanied by her adopted daughter, Quintana Roo. One day Didion visits a family cemetery, on another she visits her great aunts. After being home several days, Didion explains that she's

> paralyzed by the neurotic lassitude engendered by meeting one's past at every turn, around every corner, inside every cupboard, I go aimlessly from room to room. I decide to meet it head-on and clean out a drawer, and I spread the contents on the bed. A bathing suit I wore the summer I was seventeen. A letter of rejection from *The Nation*, an aerial photograph of the site for a shopping center my father did not build in 1954. Three teacups hand-painted with cabbage roses and signed "E. M.," my grandmother's initials. There is no final solution for letters of rejection from *The Nation* and teacups hand-painted in 1900. Nor is there any answer to snapshots of one's grandfather as a young man on skis, surveying around Donner Pass in the year 1910. I smooth out the snapshot and look into his face, and do and do not see my own.[20]

Didion's foray into the past tells no coherent or continuous story, provides no "final solution" or "answer"; she presents only a series of discrete, symbolic items as representative moments from a distant and elusive past, constituting a temporary psychological retrenchment and recognition of personal and historical loss. When Didion concludes the essay with a discussion of her daughter's birthday, she acknowledges her own loss by transferring her feelings onto a metaphorical other—her daughter—and indirectly confronting a childhood home that she can no longer call her own:

> I would like to promise her that she will grow up with a sense of her cousins and of rivers and of her great-grandmother's teacups, would like to pledge her a picnic on a river with fried chicken and her hair uncombed, would like to give her *home* for her birthday, but we live differently now and I can promise her nothing like that.[21]

In "Notes from a Native Daughter" Didion laments that the Sacramento of childhood is no longer populated by native sons and daughters. She initially registers her personal loss in social terms: the story of her generation will have little meaning to the 15,000 imported workers at Aerojet-General; "they will have lost the real past," Didion mourns, "and gained a manufactured one."[22] Didion qualifies this assessment, however, by suggesting that "perhaps it is presumptuous of me to assume that they will be missing something."[23] Her comments constitute, as Chris Anderson explains, a "rhetoric of process"; they are "highly tentative, grounded in the moment of the writing, a function of her effort at that place and time to think through a problem in language."[24] In this instance, Didion comes to the resolution that "this has been a story not about Sacramento at all, but about the things we lose and the promises we break as we grow older."[25] Didion again acknowledges the loss of her irretrievable childhood but continues to hide a personal self behind her use of the first person plural pronoun, "we." Although autobiographical writing is typically characterized by self-display, often self-glorification, Didion rarely explores her concerns in solely personal terms. Whether this patterned presentation of self derives from nature, socialization as a female, or a desire to deflect accusations of solipsism, Didion seems willing to transcend, or at least minimize, overt declarations of self by associating her loss with the loss shared by all of humanity.

Didion documents another self-revelatory moment at the conclusion of "On Keeping a Notebook." She tells the reader about the time when she first saw a "blonde in a Pucci bathing suit sitting with a couple of fat men by the pool at the Beverly Hills Hotel."[26] Several years later she sees the same

> blonde coming out of Saks Fifth Avenue in New York with her California complexion and a voluminous mink coat. In the harsh wind that day she looked old and irrevocably tired to me, and even the skins in the mink coat were not worked the way they were doing them that year, not the way she would have wanted them done, and there is a point to this story. For a while after that I did not like to look in the mirror, and my eyes would skim the newspapers and pick out only the deaths, the cancer victims, the premature coronaries, the suicides, and I stopped riding the Lexington Avenue IRT because I noticed for the first time that all the strangers I had seen for years—the man with the seeing-eye dog, the spinster who read the classified pages every day, the fat girl who always got off with me at Grand Central—looking older than they once had.[27]

Didion's awareness of "only the deaths, the cancer victims, the premature coronaries, the suicides" reveals, once again, her preoccupation with "the underside of the tapestry." Didion herself confesses that "I tend to always look for the wrong side, the bleak side. I have since I was a child."[28] While this constituent and metaphorical reading of the world links childhood and adult selves and provides a patterned continuity throughout her works, Didion also reveals a crisis of self that requires her to confront the idealized world of childhood, as she does in "John Wayne: A Love Song," and finally reject it in favor of a more adult perspective of self and its world.

Didion's preoccupation with childhood and children informs not only her personal essays but her cultural criticism as well. In "Where the Kissing Never Stops," for example, Didion's thinly veiled criticism of Joan Baez is predicated in part on the folk singer's naive idealism. At the Institute for the Study of Nonviolence, under the tutelage of Baez and Ira Sandperl—"who has, all his life, followed some imperceptibly but fatally askew rainbow"[29]—the young students do ballet exercises and listen to Beatles records, spend afternoons in total silence, and, among other things, "worry a great deal about 'responding to one another with beauty and tenderness.'"[30] Baez has good intentions but she is, self-admittedly, politically naive. Though Didion acknowledges, as we shall see, the importance of psychological and real escape, Baez and her students (children) retreat into an Edenic world and refuse to acknowledge the responsibilities and harsher realities of adult life. The Institute for the Study of Nonviolence is a place, Didion explains, "where the sun shines and the ambiguities can be set aside a little while longer, a place where everyone can be warm and loving and share confidences."[31]

Though Didion spent time at the Institute for the Study of Nonviolence, she does not include her journalistic self as a principal character in the piece. She presents material through a disembodied voice that only obliquely reveals her personal convictions and beliefs. Didion's preoccupation with childhood and adult selves—with the past and the present, the ideal and the real—is revealed in her criticism of Baez. This detached journalistic self might seem to underscore Didion's objectivity, but it in fact reflects, as it does in Wolfe's writing, the personal values and beliefs that separate the author from her subjects. However, while Didion is critical—at times harshly critical—of Baez and other subjects, she nonetheless "creates reader sympathy for her view" by acknowledging that she herself is not "completely free of the errors she criticizes in others."[32]

Didion is also suspicious of collective action and group behavior; she explains in "On the Morning After the Sixties," the penultimate chapter in *The White Album*, that she belongs "to a generation distrustful of political highs."[33] "The personal," she adds, "was all most of us expected to find.

We would make a separate peace . . . do graduate work in Middle English" and "survive outside history."[34] While Didion cannot literally exist outside of history, as a journalist she has survived, even thrived, outside the events she witnesses and records. Her belief in the primacy and integrity of a personal self, rather than a socially constituted and politically conscious one, is tangibly dramatized in her journalistic role as detached observer. This "physical" distance represents, in fact, an ideological position. The alternative lifestyle of the counterculture, as we saw in "Where the Kissing Never Stops," is a challenge to a system of values—rooted in a frontier ethic and in 1950s America—that Didion firmly endorses. Like McPhee, Didion presents a self firmly grounded in the values and beliefs of a traditional and mythic America. McPhee, however, articulates an authentic American self (i.e. American Adam) that symbolically retreats into a utopian and ficticious past, whereas Didion more readily questions the viability of such identity formations. This is underscored repeatedly in "Slouching Towards Bethlehem," a critical account of life in the Haight-Ashbury district of San Francisco during the 1967 "Summer of Love."

Didion begins the essay with a catalogue of societal problems and then focuses on the atomization of the family and the plight of our children:

> The center was not holding. It was a country of bankruptcy notices and public-auction announcements and commonplace reports of casual killings and misplaced children and abandoned homes and vandals who misspelled even the four-letter words they scrawled. It was a country in which families routinely disappeared, trailing bad checks and repossession papers. Adolescents drifted from city to torn city, sloughing off both the past and the future as snakes shed their skins, children who were never taught and would never now learn the games that had held the society together. People were missing. Children were missing. Parents were missing. Those left behind filed desultory missing-persons reports, then moved on themselves.[35]

At the time, many of these missing persons, adolescents and young adults, gravitated to Haight-Ashbury, the hippie Mecca of America that was criticized in Nicholas Von Hoffman's New Journalism work *We Are the People Our Parents Warned Us Against* (1967) and eulogized almost twenty years later in Charles Perry's journalistic history *The Haight-Ashbury* (1984). Didion dramatizes, in a series of scenes and vignettes, the problems she identifies in her introduction. Most all of her characters are naive, self-indulgent, and socially irresponsible. Katherine Usher Henderson explains that readers finally realize "that all of the hippies are emotionally stunted; they are essentially children playing at being grown-ups.

They fulfill their most elemental needs—for food, companionship, and sexual release—but they avoid all the complexities of adult life."[36] While most all of the principal characters are indeed child-like, Didion is particularly interested in adolescents and children. In the penultimate section Didion introduces a five-year-old girl who is high on acid. In the final section she recounts a story of a three-year-old boy who started a fire and burned his arm while the adults were sleeping. Later, when the boy's mother shows her questionable concern for her son—she yells at him because he is chewing on an electric cord—the other adults are more interested in retrieving "some very good Moroccan hash which had dropped down through a floor board damaged in the fire."[37] Didion, of course, is critical of these "adults," much in the way Joe McGinniss is critical of authority figures in his nonfiction. When the parents are "missing," they both seem to be saying, what hope do the children have? Without the real and symbolic authority of parents, the guidelines of family and a traditional value structure, we all become, in a sense, misplaced children. When Didion writes about Joan Baez and her students, about her own daughter, and about other (missing) children, we hear echoes of her own past and childhood, acknowledgment of personal loss registered, once again, in social and metaphorical terms.

Didion does occasionally acknowledge her journalistic presence in "Slouching Towards Bethlehem," as well as identify her beliefs in brief but key personal statements. But because she cultivates a seemingly "objective" and neutral voice and uses the present tense to dramatize her material in a series of reconstructed scenes—she shows rather than tells—her portrait of Haight-Ashbury initially appears untainted by either a personal bias or a specific authorial perspective. Yet, Didion's preoccupation with a real and symbolic childhood reveals, as I noted, the intensely personal and metaphorical dimensions of this and other works of social criticism. Didion's appropriation of the social world, I would argue, represents an intersection of private and public domains. She refuses to compromise her individuality or re-evaluate the integrity of her personal beliefs by defining a public self in relation to either a social collective or cause, whether it is Baez's Institute for the Study of Nonviolence or the alternative lifestyle of the counterculture. Though "Slouching Towards Bethlehem" is often identified as an exemplary piece of nonfiction writing, it is compromised, as is much of Tom Wolfe's writing, by the author's inability to get close enough to her subjects to see the world on their own idiosyncratic terms. Didion does not so much explore the lives of her subjects as reject them; the material world vitiates in an uncompromising deference to a personal and metaphorical reality, a reality that is occasionally characterized, as we shall see, by a physical and psychological retreat from society.

In *Style as Argument: Contemporary American Nonfiction*, Chris Anderson maintains that the "grammar" of Didion's writing is the "rhetoric of particularity." "She is incapable," Anderson adds, "of thinking 'in abstracts' or traveling in the 'world of idea.' "[38] While Didion does indeed ground her work in the particular, concrete details of contemporary American life, these details are, in fact, the physical manifestation of a symbolic idealist who places ideas above the reality they allegedly signify. Didion herself acknowledges that "my adult life has been a succession of expectations, misconceptions. I dealt only with an idea I had of the world, not with the world as it was."[39]

For a person who has difficulty confronting, or recognizing, "the world as it is," it might seem surprising that Didion would choose journalism as a profession; after all, she must confront a very "real" world populated with "real" human beings. Didion explains, however, that she often altered her journalism routine in order to compensate for her inability to function in certain social and professional contexts. She elaborates:

> I'm not sure that people who write had much sense of themselves as the center of the room when they were children. I think the way people work often comes out of their weaknesses, out of their failings. In my case, I wasn't a very good reporter. If I got into a town where a story was and I found a *Life* team there, I'd go home. So I had somehow to come out of every story having *interpreted* it, because I wasn't going to get it from anybody else.[40]

In the preface to *Slouching Towards Bethlehem*, Didion candidly acknowledges a similar fear of certain social encounters:

> I am bad at interviewing people. I avoid situations in which I have to talk to anyone's press agent. . . . I do not like to make telephone calls, and would not like to count the mornings I have sat on some Best Western motel bed somewhere and tried to force myself to put through the call to the assistant district attorney.[41]

She adds that "my only advantage as a reporter is that I am so physically small, so temperamentally unobtrusive, and so neurotically inarticulate that people tend to forget that my presence runs counter to their best interests."[42]

Didion's comments about reporting reveal a preoccupation with journalism processes and forms that characterizes much of the best literary nonfiction: Hunter S. Thompson's *Hell's Angels*, Michael Herr's *Dis-*

patches, and, among others, Timothy Crouse's *The Boys on the Bus*. More specifically, Didion implicitly suggests that the problematic author-subject relationship is in part defined by authorial betrayal. As Janet Malcolm underscores throughout *The Journalist and the Murder*, the prospective subject of a journalism story would typically interpret Didion's demeanor and other seemingly sympathetic gestures as signs of the author's goodwill. Didion's self-effacing manner and non-threatening presence may disarm subjects and encourage them to disclose information that more assertive journalists might be unable to elicit. Subjects often fail to realize, however, that the journalist is ultimately "a kind of confidence man"—in this instance, a confidence woman—"preying on people's vanity, ignorance, or loneliness, gaining their trust and betraying them without remorse,"[43] as Didion, Wolfe, and McGinniss often seem to do. "The disparity between what seems to be the intention of an interview as it is taking place and what it actually turns out to have been," Malcolm explains, "always comes as a shock to the subject."[44] Didion also explains that it is really impossible to describe people, including friends, in terms that are flattering, for the writer's perception of them never fully corresponds with their images of themselves.[45]

Didion's comments also suggest, however, that the public nature of journalism may elicit unacknowledged reservations of personal identity. Didion's social reserve might be interpreted as a form of self-censorship, an unwillingness to claim a portion of public space typically reserved for and dominated by men. Didion's positioning of her journalistic self as a detached observer and interpreter of experience might implicitly reveal, in other words, her ideological position in an oppressive, patriarchal culture. As Albert Stone notes in his discussion of women's autobiographies, "Women authors are not always explicit about the victimization embedded in their own stories."[46] Not surprisingly, Didion rarely assumes, perhaps because of her social anxiety, the role of participatory journalist. Her alleged dislike of social interaction prevents her from getting "inside" her characters and reporting (like Gay Talese) on their private thoughts and feelings. She often relies on symbolic details (like Tom Wolfe) to illuminate the lives and lifestyles of her characters.

Didion even reveals a desire to separate herself from social others—"to live outside of history," as she explains in "On the Morning After the Sixties." This is dramatized, as it is in the works of McPhee, when she reports on remote and often sparsely populated places. In "Quiet Days in Malibu," for example, Didion tells the reader that "all my life I had been trying to spend time in one greenhouse or another, and all my life the person in charge of one greenhouse or another had been trying to hustle me out." When she was nine, she was told at one greenhouse that the "purchase of a nickel pansy did not entitle me to 'spend the day,' and at another that my breathing was 'using up the air.' "[47] Twenty-five years later, however, Didion discovered the greenhouse of Amado Vazquez, who "seemed willing," Didion explains, "to take only the most benign notice of my presence. He seemed to assume that I had my own reasons for being there."[48] The greenhouse and other special human structures, whether museums or dams, reveal—as does writing itself—Didion's need to find "both real and psychological defenses against a meaningless, disorderly universe."[49] These structures are also profound and recurring expressions of Didion's private self. When she reports on the expensive summer homes in Newport ("The Seacoast of Despair"), the California Governor's mansion, past and present ("Many Mansions"), and J. Paul Getty's museum ("The Getty"), she confronts these public places as a tour member (anonymous citizen) and largely eschews any form of social interaction. On occasion, of course, when Didion visits public buildings and facilities—The Operations Control Center for the California State Water Project ("Holy Water") and Hoover Dam ("At the Dam"), for example—she must interact with worker personnel. Unlike McPhee, however, who personalizes organizations, institutions, and systems by focusing on individuals, Didion reaffirms, perhaps unconsciously, her belief in the sanctity of a private self by leaving "characters" nameless or by identifying them as merely bureaucrats or "systems" people. Though Didion does identify the three remaining residents at Alcatraz Island ("The Rock")—one of them, former prison guard John Hart, gives her a tour of the facilities—she interprets her visit in strictly personal terms. She explains that "to like a place like" Alcatraz, as Didion does, "you have to want a moat."[50] As her confession suggests, Didion visits Alcatraz for idiosyncratic reasons, and thereby reveals a private, reclusive self who desires to exist, if only symbolically, outside of time and history. More specifically, when Didion explains "that I liked it out there" (at Alcatraz) because it was a "ruin devoid of human vanities, clean of human illusions, an empty place reclaimed by the weather,"[51] she seems to reveal an unconscious and symbolic desire to transcend, or escape from, her secular existence and physical self. Didion seems to acknowledge a similar desire in describing Hoover Dam as "a Dynamo finally free of man, splendid at last in absolute isolation, transmitting power and releasing water to a world where no one is."[52]

Her desire to divorce herself from society and thereby preserve an inviolate private self might in part be explained by gender as well as by a commitment to a Western frontier ethic. It is important to remember, however, that Didion came of age in the 1950s, a time when an expanding bureaucracy and a fear of both Communist take-over and nuclear destruction challenged, if not undermined, any notion of an imperial self. Not surprisingly, Didion reveals, as does Norman Mailer, a recurrent concern with psychic and physical survival. Her articulation of a "minimal" self might be understood as a manifestation of nuclear anxiety, an unacknowledged and perhaps unconscious fear of personal and cultural annihilation. Christopher Lasch argues that since World War II, and particularly in the last twenty years, as the world has become an increasingly dangerous place, we see the appearance of a "minimal" or "narcissistic" self—a "self uncertain of its own outlines" that longs "either to remake the world in its own image or to merge into its environment in blissful union."[53] These complementary but seemingly contradictory impulses are symbolically imbedded in the apocalyptic image of the Dynamo, which Didion describes as "free of man" and "splendid . . . in absolute isolation." Didion remakes (redefines) the human-made world (Dynamo) in her own image and articulates a transcendent identity that exists—temporarily and metaphorically—outside of secular human experience.

At the conclusion of "Rock of Ages," she even suggests that secession from society is a real possibility: "I could tell you that I came back because I had promises to keep, but maybe it was because nobody asked me to stay."[54] Didion's desire to make a separate piece is tacitly revealed in her profiles of Howard Hughes and Georgia O'Keeffe. She describes O'Keeffe, for example, as "hard, a straight shooter, a woman clean of received wisdom and open to what she sees."[55] While Didion "quietly" admires O'Keeffe's decision to separate herself from society and thus live on her own idiosyncratic and quite radical terms, the author herself does have "promises to keep": she is married and has a daughter, Quintana Roo, who was adopted the year before "Rock of Ages" was first published. Moreover, she is a journalist (and novelist). When she transcribes her experience for readers from whom she nominally wishes to divorce herself, her private self and intimate concerns are inevitably superseded by a commitment to a professional and public writing-self.

Didion's social and psychological marginalization is most vividly illustrated in key moments of *The White Album*, which was published in the same year, 1979, with two other important works of literary journalism, *The Right Stuff* and *The Executioner's Song*. If in *Slouching Towards Bethlehem* Didion reveals the difficulty of affirming continuity between childhood and adult selves, in *The White Album* she dramatizes by the act of writing the difficulty of maintaining a central coherent identity. Didion begins "The White Album," the opening piece in the collection, by saying that "we tell ourselves stories in order to live."[56] In doing so, she identifies a community of social others by using the first person plural pronoun, "we," and by acknowledging that storytelling is one of the primary ways in which we share and make public our personal experiences and perceptions of the world. In the second paragraph, however, Didion qualifies this initial declaration: "I began to doubt," she explains, "the premises of all the stories I had ever told myself."[57] Didion questions the epistemological authority of storytelling and acknowledges, by changing to the first person singular pronoun, "I," that this revelation strains, if not severs, the social bonds shared with others. On the following page, Didion elaborates on her dilemma:

> I was supposed to have a script, and had mislaid it. I was supposed to hear cues, and no longer did. I was meant to know the plot, but all I knew was what I saw: flash pictures in variable sequence, images with no "meaning" beyond their temporary arrangement, not a movie but a cutting room experience. In what would probably be the middle of my life I wanted still to believe in the narrative and in the narrative's intelligibility, but to know that one could change the sense with every cut was to begin to perceive the experience as rather more electrical than ethical.[58]

These initial comments, all from the first section, establish the epistemological and personal frame through which we interpret what follows. In most general terms, "The White Album" is a "story of the sixties, a story with a beginning and an end, but no plot, no moral, no rationally motivated characters."[59] Didion builds the piece around an accretion of images, moments, and scenes—"flash cuts"—that seem to have "no 'meaning' beyond their temporary arrangement." While there is no recognizable narrative line, the clustering of images constitutes a number of recognizable authorial concerns, most notably a preoccupation with social disorder, random violence, and death. Didion also makes references to her own physical and psychological problems. In some respects, "The White Album" is very much like "Slouching Towards Bethlehem." The principal difference is in the way Didion articulates and deploys a writing self. In "Slouching Towards Bethlehem" Didion presents, on the one hand, a journalistic self in search of a story. Her presence is most strongly felt, however, in her vivid dramatization of character and scene. Though the social world around her may be breaking down, she is capable, as a writer, of temporarily yoking and controlling this disorder in language.

In "The White Album," however, Didion articulates a crisis of self by dramatizing her inability to make sense of the world—the late 1960s—that is ostensibly falling apart around her. The piece is punctuated with metadiscursive comments that both question the means we use to understand experience and acknowledge Didion's inability, or refusal, to make absolute, or even tentative, interpretations of that experience. While a writer like Hunter S. Thompson willingly embraces disorder and experiments with fragmented narrative forms, Didion seems to have more difficulty adapting to a changing social environment. Didion explains, for example, that she "watched Robert Kennedy's funeral on a verandah at the Royal Hawaiian Hotel in Honolulu, and also the first reports from My Lai." She also read "the story of Betty Landsdown Fouquet, a 26-year-old woman with faded blond hair who put her five-year-old daughter out to die on the center divider of Interstate 5 some five miles south of the last Bakersfield exit."[60] She repeatedly indicates that these and other events did not fit into any narrative that she knew. Didion is hesitant about what these images mean, or what they could possibly suggest. As a transition to the next section, she simply states: "Another flash cut." The gaps and "silences"—between paragraph and sections—suggest, as does the metaphor of the "white ablum" itself, a kind of literary paralysis, a refusal or inability to make connections between bits of social phenomena.

Didion's crisis, of course, is personal as well as epistemological; she is psychologically separated from a social world she cannot fully understand. In the seventh section of "The White Album," Didion provides a list of items she had taped inside her closet in Hollywood during a period when she worked regularly as a reporter. The list reads:

To Pack and Wear:
  2 *skirts*
  2 *jerseys or leotards*
  1 *pullover sweater*
  2 *pairs shoes*
  stockings
  bra
  nightgown, robe, slippers
  cigarettes
  bourbon
  bag with:
    shampoo
    toothbrush and paste
    Basis soap

razor, deodorant
aspirin, prescriptions, Tampax
face cream, powder, baby oil

To Carry:
mohair throw
typewriter
2 legal pads and pens
files
house keys[61]

Didion explains that this list was made by a person "who prized control . . . someone determined to play her role as if she had the script, heard the cues, knew the narrative."[62] Didion goes on to explain that there is one significant omission in this list: a watch. Didion had skirts, jerseys, leotards, legal pads, pens, files, and a house key but still did not know, metaphorically speaking, what time it was. Didion reveals here and in the following passage that her personal dislocation was concealed by, and out of touch with, commitment to a socially recognizable role. Didion notes that between the years 1966 and 1971, "I appeared, on the face of it, a competent enough member of some community or another, a signer of contracts and Air Travel cards, a citizen: I wrote a couple of times a month for one magazine or another, published two books, worked on several motion pictures; participated in the paranoia of the time, in the raising of a small child."[63] Didion adds that "this was an adequate enough performance, as improvisations go. The only problem was that my entire education, everything I had ever been told or had told myself, insisted that the production was never meant to be improvised."[64] Didion, who came of age during the conservative Eisenhower years, feels incapable as a person and writer of dealing with the cultural fragmentation and social change of the 1960s. Her personal crisis is most tangibly revealed in a page-long transcription from her psychiatric report:

In June of this year patient experienced an attack of vertigo, nausea, and a feeling that she was going to pass out. . . . Emotionally, patient has alienated herself almost entirely from the world of other human beings. Her fantasy life appears to have been virtually completely preempted by primitive, regressive libidinal preoccupations many of which are distorted and bizarre. . . . Patient's thematic productions on the Thematic Apperception Test emphasize her fundamentally pessimistic, fatalistic, and depressive view of the world around her. It is as though she feels deeply that all human effort is foredoomed to failure, a conviction which seems to push her further into a dependent, passive withdrawal. In her view she lives in a world of people moved by strange, conflicted, poorly comprehended, and, above all, devious motivations which commit them inevitably to conflict and failure.[65]

The psychiatric report represents a professional and putatively accurate assessment of a personal crisis that usurps Didion's own power of self-definition. Her response to her illness, as well as to the life circumstances surrounding it, are allegedly discredited by the formal and objective—scientific—psychiatric diagnosis. Yet, her presentation of an incapacitated self, which occurs on more than one occasion in both *Slouching Towards Bethlehem* and *The White Album*, is also an artful persona that allows her to identify and represent social breakdown in personal and metaphorical terms while simultaneously affirming her integrity as a journalist. Didion's candid acknowledgment of her own problems—she has nothing to hide—suggests that she will speak with equal candor and honesty about other subjects.

Moreover, though Didion's psychiatric report might initially be read as "a paradigm of personal incapacitation—offered also as an image of cultural breakdown or a general emblem of existential paralysis"—it "becomes instead a point of literary departure, initiating rather than terminating narrative possibilities."[66] Whereas John McPhee and Tom Wolfe create an impression of control by concealing discordant elements in their personal lives and journalism procedures, Didion willingly dramatizes her literary and personal "problems" by articulating a post-modern self in a process of constant becoming. Though perhaps incapable of fully coming to terms with the world around her, Didion still can cogently articulate the process of her failure. As the following and concluding comment of the section indicates, however, Didion does indeed come to terms with (years later) this crisis from her past: "By way of comment I offer only that an attack of vertigo and nausea does not now seem to me an inappropriate response to the summer of 1968."[67] An older and more "objective" Didion looks back, as she so often does in *Slouching Towards Bethlehem*, to redefine a dislocated private self in social and public terms—as a barometer of the time—and unite it with a more recent, and seemingly healthy, personal identity. "The White Album" tells "the story of the sixties from the perspective of a woman who has banished the demons of the nightmare through the written record of their devastation."[68]

While the metadiscursive nature of "The White Album" underscores Didion's epistemological and personal crises, her willingness to discuss and make her concerns public reveals a need to make at least tentative sense of a disorderly universe and a dislocated personal identity. The metaphor of the white album is, of course, an allusion to the Beatles' record from the late 1960s, and like Alcatraz and Hoover Dam, it represents, in Didion's world, a symbolic icon empty of meaning, "devoid of human vanities" and "clean of human illusions." But it also suggests the possibility of a new beginning—a clean (blank) slate on which to articulate a more accommodating vision of the self and its world. In the remaining pieces of *The White Album*, Didion presents herself, Katherine Usher Henderson explains, as "generally a more mellow, accepting woman."[69]

This is most tangibly revealed in "In Bed," an often-anthologized essay about migraine headaches. Didion presents an examined self in a recognizable confessional manner, revealing a concern for her physical and emotional well-being. Early in the essay she vividly describes the intense physical pain she experiences with each migraine:

> I fought migraine then, ignored the warnings it sent, went to school and later to work in spite of it, sat through lectures in Middle English and presentations to advertisers with involuntary tears running down the right side of my face, threw up in washrooms, stumbled home by instinct, emptied ice trays onto my bed and tried to freeze the pain in my right temple, wished only for a neurosurgeon who would do a lobotomy on house call, and cursed my imagination.[70]

As Didion indicates with her use of the past tense and in the first line of the following paragraph—"it was a long time before I began thinking mechanistically enough to accept migraine for what it was"[71]—she now understands her physical ailment in a significantly different way. Near the end of the essay, in fact, Didion curiously refers to her migraine "as more friend than lodger." She explains that "we have reached a certain understanding, my migraine and I."[72] Didion does not merely accept and understand it as a physical phenomenon but acknowledges that it represents an undeniable part of her identity.

It constitutes one mark of personal identity, in fact, that becomes more resonant when Didion makes similar references to other somatic and psychological illnesses. *Slouching Towards Bethlehem*, for example, is prefaced with an acknowledgment of physical illness that all but incapacitates her: "I was . . . sick as I have ever been when I was writing 'Slouching Towards Bethlehem'; the pain kept me awake at night and so for twenty and twenty-one hours a day I drank gin-and-hot-water to blunt the pain and took Dexedrine to blunt the gin and wrote the piece."[73] Prior to these confessions, Didion explains that she had "suffered a small stroke, leaving" her "apparently undamaged but actually aphasic."[74] These comments might lead readers to interpret Didion's presentation of self as a stereotypical model of female identity. That is, women are understood to be fundamentally—"naturally"—more emotional than men, and that they are first and foremost defined biologically, by their somatic selves and their reproductive ability.[75] The problem, Edwin M. Schur points out, is that "women are perceived and reacted to at least initially, and often primarily, in terms of their femaleness [and the character traits we associate with it]. Only secondarily, if at all, do their other identities and qualities determine responses to them."[76] If the dominant and socially accepted response to physical illnesses and emotional excess is, as Wolfe intimates in the previous chapter, properly masculine—keeping feelings inside—the very act of announcing one's problems, as Didion does, constitutes a form of social deviance.

While Didion does not consciously present a bio-socially determined self, one defined by sex and social prescription, her personal identity is in part defined—much more than her male counterparts—by a genuine and candid awareness of her somatic self and history. Only rarely do male literary journalists make reference to their physical selves, and when they do it is most often in relation to an external event that presents itself as a possible threat to their well-being. In *The Armies of the Night*, for example, Mailer makes the reader quite aware that the demonstration at the Pentagon could result in serious physical injury. As he charges the line of MPs, he explains that "two of them leaped on him at once in the cold clammy murderous fury of all cops at that existential moment of making their bust."[77] Male literary journalists typically shun, however, the psychological and emotional dimensions of self-exploration. McPhee and Wolfe, for example, provide personal but metaphorical readings of reality but rarely introduce private concerns and obsessions—fears, worries, desires, and so on—into their constructed worlds. Rather, they cultivate an objective journalistic self that generally conceals both private motivations and the emotional ups and downs of their nature. While it is convenient to maintain that emotional detachment is a requisite of good journalism, it might also be argued that adopting the behavior of a socially defined role—in this instance, a reporter's cool detachment—reveals, in fact, an unconscious desire to deny emotions and, thereby, define the self as an entirely rational and perhaps superior being, as is implied in Wolfe's journalistic persona. This constitutes, of course, an ideological as well as a psychological statement of self, not merely a distrust of emotions and instincts but a fear of being something other than what we stereotypically understand as masculine.

As we shall see in the following chapter, Hunter S. Thompson articulates a stereotypically masculine identity. Like Didion, Thompson frequently presents himself on the threshold of physical and emotional collapse. He largely eschews emotional exploration of these breakdowns, however, and implies that private pain and mental suffering are caused and superseded by an impersonal and punitive social world. While Didion seeks professional help and believes, at least initially, that her psychological illness originates within her, Thompson shuns professional advice and seeks to cure himself by retreating to the natural sanctuary of his Woody Creek home.

6

Hunter S. Thompson: A Ritual Reenactment of Deviant Behavior

Hunter S. Thompson grew up in "the stifling small-town atmosphere of Louisville, Kentucky."[1] His father was an insurance agent whose only amusement was going out to the track early in the morning to time the horses. As a teenager Thompson "rebelled," according to Timothy Crouse, by "knocking off" liquor stores and gas stations.[2] In one three-day period, Thompson and two friends robbed the same gas station three times. Thompson recalls standing by his apartment window—which overlooked the gas station—and watching the police investigate the burglaries while he and his friends drank beer. Thompson was also an accomplished shoplifter; he would go empty-handed, he explained, into a jewelry store and leave with a half-dozen watches. Though Thompson was never arrested, Louisville authorities "managed to put him in jail for thirty days on a phony rape charge."[3] He was eighteen at the time and very frightened by his brief period of incarceration. Though Thompson swore off a life of petty crime and decided to devote his life to writing, the articulation of a criminal (deviant) self, both real and metaphoric, would later become the cornerstone of his literary nonfiction.

Shortly after his release from jail, Thompson enlisted in the Air Force and became a sports writer for the base newspaper. He was also writing for a number of civilian papers under the pen names of "Sebastian Owl" and "Thorne Stockton." When this was discovered, he was fired from the base newspaper and threatened with duty in Iceland. Because of Thompson's general inability to conform to Air Force life, he was discharged two years before his enlistment expired. At the time, Colonel

Evans, of the Office of Information Services, made this assessment of Thompson: "This Airman, although talented, will not be guided by policy or personal advice and guidance. Sometimes his rebel and superior attitude seems to rub off on other airmen staff members. He has little consideration for military bearing or dress and seems to dislike the service and want out as soon as possible."[4]

Over the next two years, a series of similar dismissals occurred. Thompson was fired from three writing jobs: in Pennsylvania for wrecking his editor's car; in Middletown, New York for insulting an advertiser and kicking "a candy machine to death"; and at *Time* for his bad attitude.[5] Between 1959 and 1963, he worked in South America and the Caribbean as a journalist for the *National Observer* (and on occasion for the *New York Herald Tribune*). While this writing is generally more conventional than his later work, Thompson nonetheless reveals his liberal, if not radical, political beliefs and underscores his social marginality through an identification with disenfranchised others. When Thompson found himself spending too much time rolling dice at the Domino Club, a club for foreign correspondents, he decided it was time to return to the United States. His departure from the *National Observer* was eventually precipitated by a disagreement with editors over coverage of the Free Speech Movement.

For a time, Thompson worked on a novel and lived in an apartment in San Francisco with his wife, Sandy. In that same year, 1964, Carey McWilliams, editor of *The Nation*, asked him if he would do an article on the Hell's Angels for $100. Thompson accepted, recalling later that the amount he received was enough to cover the following month's rent. The article was eventually expanded, of course, into *Hell's Angels: A Strange and Terrible Saga*, in which Thompson wrote sympathetically about, and even identified with, the notorious "outlaw" motorcycle gang.

In the ensuing three years, Thompson wrote for *Pageant*, *The Distant Drummer*, and *Scanlan's Monthly*, and he later ran for Sheriff of Aspen County on the Freak Power Ticket. Thompson's tentative platform included plans to rip up city streets and replace them with sod and to restrict fishing and hunting to Aspen residents. Thompson also promised to limit his use of LSD to non-working hours. (He lost by only six votes.)

In 1970 he began his association with Jann Wenner, editor and publisher of *Rolling Stone* magazine. The relationship proved to be a mutually beneficial one. The freshness and new energy Wenner was looking for, following his 1970 purge of editors and writers, was provided by Thompson. In turn, Wenner gave Thompson the creative latitude needed to develop the "Gonzo" style that characterizes such works as *Fear and Loathing in Las Vegas* and *The Curse of Lono*. Thompson became National Affairs Editor at *Rolling Stone* in 1970, and he held the position until 1974. He continued his relationship with the magazine into the early 1980s. In more recent years, Thompson has worked in a massage parlor (doing research) and contributed a weekly column to the *San Francisco Examiner*.

In this brief biographical sketch, we can see that Thompson's "criminal" past, his early dismissal from the Air Force, as well as other problems he had keeping writing jobs, point more generally to his repudiation of authority and his refusal to conform to the behavioral dictates of a socially defined role, whether it be citizen of Louisville, enlisted Airman, or journalist. Thompson is all too willing to identify himself in opposition to virtually any cultural norm—as an "outlaw" or "deviant"—and make a public record of his felonious past: "I took that fatal dive off the straight and narrow path so long ago that I can't remember when I first become [*sic*] a felon—but I have been one ever since, and it's way too late to change now. In the eyes of The Law, my whole life has been one long and sinful felony."[6] Although Thompson's "outlaw" status seems as much chosen as conferred, it is also, as this passage suggests, a confirmation of the title ascribed to him by the normative culture. As Erving Goffman points out, the deviant can never quite escape from his past: "What often results is not the acquisition of fully normal status, but a transformation of self from someone with a particular blemish into someone with a record of having corrected a particular blemish."[7] Though Thompson has largely put an end to his criminal past, he still defines himself, throughout his nonfiction, as what he once was: a felon (i.e. outlaw, deviant). Therefore, we must first begin to interpret Thompson's work through this initial metaphor of the self, for his writings repeatedly dramatize his adversarial relationship to mainstream culture.

More specifically, in a number of works Thompson describes himself ambiguously as a fugitive on the lam, running from some undefined or questionably real authority. His flight is fueled by a paranoia that is both real and comically imagined, by a feeling of persecution that is dramatized and exaggerated for literary purposes. Thompson's story, as we shall see, is one of personal breakdown and recovery. Because he moves between the secluded and private world of his Woody Creek (Colorado) home (and other symbolic sanctuaries) and the larger world outside, it is essential that we see his writing not as a collection of individual works but as one ongoing saga of emergence and renewal, as a ritual enactment of deviant behavior in which the dynamic relation between putative outsider and the normative culture is chronicled and explored during a period of social crisis and change. In the following pages I reconstruct the essential pieces of this personal, literary, and cultural story.

To start with, Thompson's journalistic assignments might be rightfully understood as journeys that begin with the departure from the real and symbolic sanctuary of his Woody Creek home. Early in *The Curse of Lono*, Thompson explains to the reader, by way of a letter to illustrator Ralph Steadman, that "the time has come to kick ass, Ralph, even if it means coming briefly out of retirement and dealing, once again, with the public. I am also in need of a rest—for legal reasons—so I want this gig to be *easy*."[8] (He is assigned to cover the Honolulu Marathon for *Running* magazine.) Thompson's "gigs" (journalism assignments) are never easy, however, and in fact they are possibly dangerous, as he suggests in the opening pages of *Fear and Loathing: On the Campaign Trail '72*. Thompson leaves the "pastoral" and private retreat of his Woody Creek home and then comments on the public world of Washington, D.C.: "Life runs fast & mean in this town," he explains. "It's like living in an armed camp, a condition of constant fear."[9] Thompson's trepidation reveals (on a personal level) a dislike of socially defined and densely populated space and simultaneously establishes (on rhetorical and cultural levels) the central conflict of his writing: the deviant (outsider) confronting a brutal and at times punitive mainstream culture. His return to "civilization" (Washington, D.C.), he wryly notes, "was not mentioned by any of the society columnists."[10]

Though a prescribed story is assigned to Thompson, he generally rejects it in favor of a more spontaneous and less predictable alternative, or he subverts the journalism occasion and redefines the assignment on his own idiosyncratic terms. For example, before Thompson and Oscar Acosta attend the National District Attorney's Conference on Narcotics and Dangerous Drugs, chronicled in *Fear and Loathing in Las Vegas*, he discloses his plan to disrupt the aforementioned event: "Our very *presence* would be an outrage. We would be attending the conference under false pretenses and dealing, from the start, with a crowd that was convened for the stated purpose of putting people like us in jail. We *were* the Menace—not in disguise, but stone-obvious drug abusers, with a flagrantly cranked-up act that we intended to push all the way to the limit."[11] Later in the motel bar, Thompson and Acosta talk to a district attorney from Georgia. They spin an elaborate and totally fictitious tale about depraved, Manson-like sex fiends and drug addicts from California who will soon be invading the South. By the time they conclude their story, the naive D.A. is in a state of utter fear and loathing. Though Thompson and Acosta are playfully "jiving" the Georgia D.A., their presence constitutes, nonetheless, a kind of deviant "noise," a calculated and profane articulation of self that disrupts our typical interpretation of reality and replaces it, in this case, with a tale of semantic and symbolic disorder. In many respects, Thompson's "playful" antics are the equivalent, on a smaller and personal scale, of the guerilla tactics and street theater staged by adversarial groups such as the Yippies. Though Thompson's articulation of a deviant self is certainly autobiographical, the product of an allegedly criminal past, the original appearance of *Fear and Loathing in Las Vegas* in two 1971 issues of *Rolling Stone* would also be appreciated by members of a youth culture that listened to psychedelic music and experimented increasingly with hallucinogenic drugs.

In *Fear and Loathing in Las Vegas* Thompson is also sent to cover the Mint 400 motorcycle race. He is unable to see the race, however, because a cloud of dust hovers in the wake of the motorcycles. "The idea of trying to 'cover this race' in any conventional press-sense," Thompson explains, "was absurd: It was like trying to keep track of a swimming meet in an Olympic-sized pool filled with talcum powder instead of water."[12] Since he is such a vituperative critic of the conventional press, Thompson seems to suggest that mainstream journalism practices do not so much illuminate as obscure. Thompson retires to the hotel bar and, several pages later, asks himself: "Was I just roaming around these Mint Hotel escalators in a drug frenzy of some kind, or had I really come out here to Las Vegas to work on a *story*?"[13] As is often the case, Thompson is never quite sure what the story is. Over four-fifths of the way through *The Curse of Lono*, Thompson tells the reader, by way of a letter to Ralph Steadman, that he does not know what he is doing on the Kona Coast. Thompson's apparent insouciance is in part a rhetorical ploy, one example of the reportorial license both his editors and reading constituency expect: Thompson performing as the irresponsible journalist. Thompson's irresponsible behavior indeed appears to be unpremeditated and more spontaneous than other literary journalists on specific assignment. He is also reenacting, however, a personal and symbolic drama, first scripted in his youth and adolescence, that reaffirms his deviant identity in an older self. Erik Erikson explains that every person "harbors a *negative identity* as the sum of all those identifications and identity fragments which the individual had to submerge in himself as undesirable or irreconcilable." At times of personal or social crises, however, a person may not be able to control these "negative elements in a positive identity."[14] Thompson, I would argue, periodically—and quite intentionally—invokes these negative elements of personal behavior in moments of adulthood and reinvents, in a positive and symbolically autobiographical way, a psychosocial deviant self. For example, much like Norman Mailer, Thompson retains, as a journalist and person, much of the "innocence" and irreverence of youth, and his repeated anarchic behavior seems to be the metaphorical embodiment of childhood resentment against adult control and authority. This is repeatedly illustrated in his critique of traditional journalism practices.

Thompson challenges, for example, the arbitrary nature of conventional journalism forms (stories) and offers a more indeterminate reading of social and personal reality. The serendipitous nature of Thompson's journey suggests that the idea for an assignment is not so much prescribed as discovered. The story and its concomitant meanings are revealed in piecemeal fashion, as Thompson chronicles, often haphazardly, his picaresque encounters. Thompson's journalism may even be seen as a parodic quest for meaning. The epistemological assumptions that buttress conventional journalism are largely inverted or ignored. For example, Thompson frequently illustrates his general disdain for conventional journalism practices: "So this article is not going to end the way I thought it would . . . and looking back at the lead I see that it didn't even start that way either. As for the middle, I can barely remember it."[15] More specifically, Thompson criticizes journalists for their continued use of the pyramid lead; he claims that five generations of journalists have clung to its "petrified tit." But it is not merely that Thompson questions such conventional ordering of facts; he questions the factual base of non-ficitional writing itself. Much of the criticism Thompson has incurred centers on his apparently slipshod journalistic practices.

In his review of Theodore H. White's *The Making of the President 1972* and Thompson's *Fear and Loathing: On the Campaign Trail '72*, for instance, Wayne C. Booth rates each journalist according to how well he establishes credibility with the reader. "*How does he know* what he says?" Booth asks. Well, Thompson gets an 'F,' because, "shit, man, his ethos ain't no fuckin' good."[16] Booth goes on to explain that since Thompson has admittedly lied so often, he will not believe anything Thompson says unless it is corroborated by another source. Thompson, however, does not build his story, as do John McPhee and Gay Talese, on a series of referential facts—that house-of-card journalism in which one "erroneous" fact may cause the whole structure to crack if not tumble. Thompson defamiliarizes, or estranges, our understanding of conventional journalism and exposes the institutional means by which more orthodox journalists make sense out of reality. He acknowledges the "fraudulent," or fictive, nature of his enterprise, while the more conventional journalists seldom recognize their arbitrary claims of objectivity. The subjective reality (or unreality) of Thompson's world is, paradoxically, predicated on the unreliability of the participant-narrator. Thompson's work needs to be evaluated beyond inflexible rubrics of falsity and truth. Deception or dissimulation in autobiographical writing may be called "fiction or fraud," as Georges Gusdorf points out, "but its artistic value is real: there is a truth affirmed beyond the fraudulent itinerary and chronology, a truth of the man, images of himself and of the world." The writer, "for his own enchantment and that of his readers, realizes himself in the unreal."[17] While Thompson, for example, may resort to hyperbole and even make up stories—like the story he allegedly told the Georgia D.A.—we can count on him to be as "truthful" as other credible journalists. As John Hellmann explains, "Presenting journalistic events through the perceptions of this maddened, even hallucinating, persona, Thompson presents his black humorist vision of those actual events without violating their actuality."[18]

When Thompson is on an assignment, he is generally accompanied by an equally (un)reliable traveling partner: with Oscar Acosta in *Fear and Loathing in Las Vegas*, with Yail Bloor in "The Great Shark Hunt," with Ralph Steadman in "The Kentucky Derby is Decadent and Depraved," and with Gene Skinner in *The Curse of Lono*. This allows Thompson to divide his personality, as Jerome Klinkowitz points out, into "*mutually exclusive personae*":

> In *Fear and Loathing in Las Vegas* Thompson travels as himself, but arrives under the credit-card pseudonym of Raoul Duke; much of the extravagant behavior is then attributed to Duke (Thompson's own nickname), whom Thompson can properly deplore. Acting and observing at the same time, Thompson also extends his persona to a third level: bringing along his attorney, identified on the dustjacket as Oscar Zeta Acosta, who in the book is made to perform the more outrageous acts which Thompson can amplify and extend by his own expressions of horror and disgust.[19]

Thompson's personal and contextual association with various sidekicks also invokes the pattern of male bonding found in much American popular culture and, as well, reaffirms his inclusion in an exclusive masculine world. Thompson and his partners' picaresque encounters reveal, not surprisingly, "the traditional American hero's reluctance to become involved with the females whom he encounters on his travels."[20] In *Fear and Loathing in Las Vegas*, for example, Oscar Acosta meets a mentally unstable young woman named Lucy and then brings her back to the hotel room. When her alleged psychosis is exacerbated by drugs they supply, Acosta and Thompson are quick to assume that she will be not merely a burden but also directly responsible for getting them in trouble with either the police or hotel management. In *The Curse of Lono*, as I noted, Thompson is assigned to cover the Honolulu marathon. He reveals, after twenty-nine pages, that he is accompanied by his fiancée. She remains unnamed, however. When Thompson meets up with his old friend, Gene Skinner, he leaves his fiancée at the hotel while they begin a series of wild and serendipitous adventures involving fishing, native-"bashing," and, of course, drinking. Thompson's fiancée reappears only occasionally in the image of a contemporary Dame Van Winkle, who is either calling Thompson a "bastard" and a "drunken sot" or criticizing him for his irresponsible and callous behavior. Because Thompson so uniformly criticizes the people he encounters on his travels and, simultaneously, cultivates a journalistic self who uses aggression and verbal insult as forms of self-survival, it seems hardly fair to identify his actions as intentionally sexist. Yet, these examples seem freighted with an unexpressed anxiety about the alleged role women play in domesticating men. At the very least, in reporting on subjects such as the Hell's Angels and national politics, Thompson constructs and reaffirms, perhaps unintentionally, an exclusive male society. Many works of American literary journalism are, in fact, a celebration and affirmation of various masculine worlds: for example, Talese's study of the Bonanno mafia family, Wolfe's examination of the space program, Plimpton's forays into sports, and Herr's chronicle of marines in Vietnam. In exploring these worlds, Thompson and other literary journalists reaffirm their generic male identities and reinforce traditionally masculine gender roles by inadequately examining the ideological underpinnings of these exclusive male societies.

Thompson's exclusion of women and his eventual flight from society may reveal, as it did in the lives of some "Beat" writers, not merely a rejection of a crass material culture but also a refusal to accept certain adult responsibilities and an inability to have a traditional relationship with a member of the opposite sex. To be fair to Thompson, however, his symbolic, if not real, exclusion of women is at least in part a calculated rhetorical strategy underscoring his social marginality. Thompson seems to believe in the sovereignty of an imperial and perhaps a male self and adamantly spurns any pro-social "forces" that threaten his independence.

Throughout his work, in fact, Thompson repeatedly dramatizes the precarious existence of this autonomous self. It is often not clear, however, why he is affected and even victimized so severely when he leaves the sanctuary of his Colorado home and reenters society. Thompson often relies on superficial cultural observations to explain his behavior and personal transformation. He too readily asserts, or suggests, that American culture is merely a harsh and punitive one, based on and perverted by a predatory capitalist system. Thompson's deficiency as a cultural critic centers on his refusal to adequately discuss the causes of his personal behavior. In *Fear and Loathing in Las Vegas*, for example, Raoul Duke (Thompson) says "I am *tired*! I'm scared, I'm crazy. This culture has beaten me down."[21] In "The Kentucky Derby is Decadent and Depraved" Thompson explains that he and Steadman are victims of "culture shock." And in *The Curse of Lono* the Kona Coast weather, persistent wind and rain, is even advanced as an explanation for Thompson's anti-social behavior. In some instances, he more specifically acknowledges that he is changed by the people about whom he writes. Sixty-six pages into *Hell's Angels*, for example, Thompson explains that he has become "so involved in the outlaw scene that" he "was no longer sure whether" he "was doing research on the Hell's Angels or being slowly absorbed by them."[22] By the conclusion of "The Kentucky Derby is Decadent and Depraved," Thompson's transformation and identification with the "other" is complete:

> Huge Pontiac Ballbuster blowing through traffic on the expressway. . . . The journalist is driving, ignoring his passenger who is now nearly naked after taking off most of his clothing, which he holds out the window, trying to wind-wash the Mace out of it. His eyes are bright red and his face and chest are soaked with the beer he's been using to rinse the awful chemical off his flesh. . . . The journalist rams the big car through traffic and into a spot in front of the terminal, then he reaches over to open the door on the passenger's side and shoves the Englishman out, snarling: "Bug off, you worthless faggot! You twisted pigfucker! [Crazed laughter.] If I weren't sick I'd kick your ass all the way to Bowling Green—you scumsucking foreign geek. Mace is too good for you. . . . We can do without your kind in Kentucky."[23]

Having used the first person throughout the piece, Thompson refers to himself as the "journalist" in the conclusion. This self-distancing is one of the few instances in which the disembodied voice of the narrator is distinctly separated from Thompson the social actor. Thompson acknowledges that his personal (core) self is threatened, even usurped, by an extrinsically determined social self and identifies the chauvinistic and potentially destructive dimensions of a culture that not only shapes his behavior but symbolically rejects him when his alter-ego and traveling partner, Ralph Steadman, is driven from society. Thompson seems unable, perhaps unwilling, to compromise his personal self and accept the self-alienation that occurs with being part of a larger social unit. Thompson's crises of self repeatedly underscore Richard Poirier's point about the difficulty of "organizing a self and a destiny for a self within the contexts that impose a self and a destiny."[24] Thompson's picture of society is, in the end, an anti-cultural statement bolstered by a nihilistic despair. A stable sense of self—his ego identity—is neither created nor confirmed by his interaction with other social beings. In fact, the survival of self is predicated upon turning himself into a beast, a monster reincarnation of the society that defines him, as Barbara Lounsberry explains,[25] and later escaping from this coercive social order. Seemingly, the only healthy self is a solitary one.

While Thompson's journalistic and metaphorical selves teeter on the brink of absorption by mainstream culture, he also defines himself as a countercultural model, an emblematic figure who endorses and gives life to a repertoire of unorthodox practices and beliefs. Conservative journalists, public officials, and certain literary critics dislike Thompson (or his work) because he carefully disobeys social rules and assumptions of conventional journalism that define appropriate behavior and signify how reality and truth are (or might be) defined. Thompson, for example, scorns the Protestant work ethic and its commitment to purposeful tasks by cultivating a lifestyle that reveals a desire to live for the moment. Thompson, furthermore, challenges the limits of consciousness, as well as the limits of the law, with his use of drugs. Whether inhabiting the physical space of his Woody Creek home or the psychic space of LSD, Thompson thrives in this marginal area that exists between civilization and anarchy. Thompson, as a romantic, feels most alive when the self exists precariously between ecstasy and annihilation, when he takes his body to the "Edge," as he calls it, through taking drugs or driving big, fast, powerful motorcycles. Thompson, for example, describes one motorcycle ride he took on a deserted stretch of highway:

> With the throttle screwed on there is only the barest margin, and no room at all for mistakes. It has to be done right . . . and that's when the strange music starts, when you stretch your luck so far that fear becomes exhilaration and vibrates along your arms. You can barely see at a hundred; the tears blow back so fast that they vaporize before they get to your ears. The only sounds are wind and a dull roar floating back from the mufflers. You watch the white line and try to lean with it . . . howling through a turn to the right, then to the left and down the long hill to Pacifica . . . letting off now, watching for cops, but only until the next dark stretch and another few seconds on . . . The Edge. . . . There is no honest way to explain it because the only people who really know where it is are the ones who have gone over. The others—the living—are those who pushed their

control as far as they felt they could handle it, and then pulled back, or slowed down, or did whatever they had to when it came time to choose between Now and Later.[26]

Thompson lives for today as if there will be no tomorrow, as the passage suggests. Thompson himself has said, on more than one occasion, that he had lived six or seven lives by the time he was twenty-seven and "with a sense of doom, a conviction that he should never have lived past thirty."[27] On a textual level, having lived six or seven lives has its correlative in the symbolic deaths and renewals Thompson experiences each time he re-enters society and later retreats from it. Though Thompson's compulsion to destroy the self is the result of an excessive and irresponsible lifestyle, it is also, paradoxically, a mechanism of survival, a way of coping with, and shielding himself from, the normative culture. That is, the use of drugs breaks down control of reason and liberates social inhibitions while it simultaneously contributes to the erosion of ego boundaries that began with Thompson's contact with a punitive social order.

In "Autobiography as the Presentation of Self for Social Immortality" Irving Louis Horowitz explains that autobiographical writing is a "social injunction"—not merely a literary event—that gives instruction to others about "how one should conduct the 'good' and avoid the 'bad' influences of that society."[28] Thompson, however, cultivates a model of "otherness" and extols certain patterns of behavior and codes of dress—signs of identity—that society deems inappropriate or improper. In *Fear and Loathing: On the Campaign Trail '72*, for example, he explains that "my garb and general demeanor is not considered normal by Washington standards. Levis don't make it in this town. . . . This is particularly true at high level press conferences, where any deviation from standard journalistic dress is considered rude and perhaps even dangerous."[29] He announces similarly that he was the only campaign reporter who was an "openly hostile Peace Freak . . . the only one who'd . . . smoke grass on Nixon's big Greyhound press bus, and certainly the only one who habitually referred to the candidate as the 'Dingbat.' "[30] On the one hand, Thompson's annunciation of deviance does not necessarily discredit him as we might expect. In fact, it constitutes a unique identity peg, a self-acknowledged token of his stigma. That is, for example, in identifying "trademark fetishes," a "love for Wild Turkey bourbon, exotic cars, powerful handguns, the Vincent Black Shadow motorcycle, Doberman pinschers, drugs, extremely amplified music, and violent rhetoric,"[31] Thompson at once affirms a masculine identity and deliberately projects an image of self that affirms his deviant status.

More specifically, Thompson plays the trickster figure who intentionally—and at times unintentionally—disrupts the social order or shows his disdain for certain persons while he underscores his role as deviant or putative outsider. Thompson thus enacts much of the playful and passsive-aggressive posturing that characterized the behavior of the counterculture, most notably the Yippies. In *Fear and Loathing: On the Campaign Trail '72*, for example, Thompson writes that he lent his press badge to a stranger who later got obnoxiously drunk and disrupted the Muskie campaign train. On another occasion, he explains that he boarded a press bus and sat behind a conservative journalist, James Kilpatrick, and began mumbling about doing hits of acid until the journalist finally retreated to the back of the bus. Thompson not only plays the trickster but tacitly acknowledges his awareness of the role he is playing. The audience, of course, is familiar with Thompson's use of drugs and he plays to this awareness by projecting an image others have come to expect, if not fully understand. He no longer needs to actually use drugs, for he has internalized this role and wears the mask that represents the concept embraced by these shared acts. As performer, he underplays certain real-life activities, facts, and characteristics while underscoring others that are compatible with this "idealized" version of the self. The alleged spontaneity of Thompson's behavior undergoes, paradoxically, "a certain bureaucratization of the spirit." The "variable impulses" of Thompson's all-too-human self are redefined in social and literary terms in order that he "give a perfectly homogeneous performance at every appointed time."[32] In other words, while Thompson voluntarily offers symbols of his marginality, they may very well represent how the deviant has internalized the culture's perception of how he should dress and behave.

As outlaw and cultural outsider, Thompson characteristically emphasizes his feelings of paranoia and guilt, which generally increase (usually at the end of a story) when his behavior gets more frantic and unpredictable. In *Fear and Loathing in Las Vegas* and "The Great Shark Hunt," as well as in *The Curse of Lono*, Thompson sees himself as a fugitive pursued by a questionably real authority. Part of Thompson's fear and paranoia may be legitimate; there are, for instance, unpaid hotel bills, purported or actual trashings of hotel rooms, a questionable line of credit, and extravagant living expenses his sponsor may not cover. Thompson is not only burdened by paranoia and guilt but believes these responses must be transparent to others. At the conclusion of "The Great Shark Hunt," Thompson and Yail Bloor arrive at the Monterey Airport and are immediately asked, over the Public Address System, to report to the Immigration Desk, where they are met by a small, muscular policeman. Since the two have been drinking and taking illegal substances, Thompson refers to the cop as their "accuser," and acknowledges that their "gig" is up. As is usually the case, Thompson is not caught—in fact he was not actually pursued. The policeman intended only to help them make their connecting flight more quickly. In *Fear and Loathing in Las Vegas*, Thompson even imagines that he and Oscar Acosta are brought to trial and charged for crimes they did not commit.

On one level, Thompson's paranoia accurately captures the feeling shared by many countercultural figures in the late 1960s and early 1970s. In addition, while Thompson's feelings of paranoia, guilt, and persecution may have originated in his criminal past, they are revealed here as a metaphor of self to be dramatized for literary purposes. Thompson, of course, is seldom chased and never apprehended by the law. Yet, the reader is led to believe that his capture is an imminent possibility. Frequently, as in "The Great Shark Hunt," the imagined chase occurs near the story's conclusion and functions as a climax to the piece. The reader wonders: Will Thompson escape? These flights from authority also confirm his outsider status and simultaneously ritualize the manner in which deviants are disposed of. Thompson is not only a symbolic challenge or threat to the social order; he has also internalized the cultural process of social control by acting as both jury and judge to crimes that he may or may not have committed. The final punishment, of course, is expulsion from society, which Thompson himself fosters by his self-conscious acts of deviance. Thompson may not only be encoding allegedly autobiographical events in a recognizable storyline but also symbolically enacting the role of punishing and authoritative adult that is so often part of deviant personalities.

Thompson's personal breakdowns are often most tangibly dramatized as he attempts to complete an assignment. His representative deterioration is reflected in, and part of, the storyline. Two-thirds of the way through "The Kentucky Derby is Decadent and Depraved," when all hell is breaking loose, Thompson loses control of narrative coherence and provides readers only bits and scraps from his notebook. "My notes and recollections from Derby Day," Thompson explains, "are somewhat scrambled."[33] Frequently, we learn of Thompson's desperate condition in an "Editor's Note." From *Fear and Loathing in Las Vegas*: "*At this point in the chronology, Dr. Duke appears to have broken down completely; the original manuscript is so splintered that we were forced to seek out the original tape recording and transcribe it verbatim.*"[34] Thompson suggests that the narrator self, like the actor self, is no longer in control. In fact, the insertion of an editorial note suggests that Thompson the author or person is no longer in control.

On the one hand, Thompson identifies the personal and metaphorical breakdowns for dramatic reasons. He heightens the conflict between himself (as deviant) and mainstream culture and intensifies the reading experience by suggesting that his survival—at least his health—is literally in question. In addition, he makes readers aware that the enterprise has been both "salvaged" and subverted by his performance as "outlaw" journalist and "psychotic" cultural critic. Thompson often parodies journalism writing, and thereby acknowledges the expendability of such endeavors while he suggests, perhaps paradoxically, that writing is the final, or only, testament of selfhood. In the finishing process, for example, Thompson frequently asserts that the copy he is "pounding" out is at best spontaneous and unedited and at worst "the most desperate last-minute hamburger jobs in the history of journalism."[35] Thompson parodies the harried journalist working under deadline pressure and testifies to the "gibberish" produced under such circumstances, thereby criticizing one of the constraints of mainstream journalism. He leads the reader to believe that his stories end simply because of editorial demands. Thompson finds himself inextricably caught up in a system he desires to criticize and separate himself from. Thompson very self-consciously comments on the limitations of journalism, and in so doing is able to exercise a certain freedom within a medium that militates against creative indulgence. This helps to explain the frequent digressions, and his acknowledgment of those digressions, that punctuate Thompson's work. It is another way to press the limits of the form. "Jesus! Another tangent, and right up front, this time—the whole *lead*, in fact, completely fucked."[36] As Hellmann explains, Thompson keeps "nearly constant focus upon his narrator's consciousness; he never lets the reader forget that he is sitting at a desk in a definite place, composing the account while fully aware of the conditions under which he writes."[37] As we move toward the end of a text, we become increasingly aware that his writing is a verbal performance, a self-reflexive process rather than a codification of significance about a subject beyond the text. The "unique value" of this kind of writing, Richard Poirier explains, "is that it can elucidate its own expendability, as more pompous forms of fiction-making [and journalism] . . . cannot."[38]

After Thompson finishes an assignment, it is necessary for him to spend time recuperating in the isolation of his Woody Creek home or in some other symbolic sanctuary. At the end of *The Curse of Lono*, for example, Thompson explains that because of his erratic behavior—and because he has proclaimed himself to be the reincarnation of the Hawaiian God Lono—the natives decide to expel him from society. Thompson, imagining once again that he is being chased—in this instance, by hired thugs—

retreats to the mythic City of Refuge, where he lives in isolation and promises to write his life story. In identifying with Lono—the God of excess and abundance, an appropriate alter-ego—Thompson self-consciously parodies his status as a mythic figure.

On a social level, Thompson's escape from society, particularly in his earlier works, coincides with the counterculture's rural retreat in the early 1970s. Moreover, it invokes the mythic American Adam who must free himself from the complications and injustices of an allegedly corrupt society in order to preserve and reaffirm an imperial, male self. While Thompson's persona shares similar traits with other American heroes and anti-heroes, he parodies the myth of the American Adam and encodes his experiences in the form of quest narratives that have little, if any, meaning. Traditionally, the quester's physical journey represents a psychological search for identity. The circular pattern of the journey and narrative reflects an integrated world view and affirms an identifiable value system shared by a community of others. Thompson begins his journey in pursuit of the unknown—he does not know what the real story is—and returns home no more enlightened than when he left. Unlike the tight, circular structure of the traditional quest narrative, Thompson's work becomes more loose and fragmented as he attempts to bring it to a close. The erosion of the storyline coincides with Thompson's own breakdown. For Thompson, the quester's experience is not so much the means by which self-discovery takes place, in which identity is created or confirmed, as it is the means by which the personal and metaphorical selves are obviated or destroyed by a punitive and destructive social order.

7

The Armies of the Night: Norman Mailer's Performing Self

Of all the recognized—and, in some instances, canonized—literary journalists, Norman Mailer is the most celebrated—and criticized. He has aggressively cultivated a familiar and not altogether favorable public image and simultaneously revealed a concern about his reputation that makes Tom Wolfe's preoccupation with literary status seem mild in comparison. Mailer's literary career began in 1948 with the publication of his naturalistic novel of World War II, *The Naked and the Dead.* In a passage from *Advertisements for Myself*, Mailer explains how this initial achievement changed his life irrevocably:

> *Never again would I know, in the dreary way one usually knows such things, what it was like to work at a dull job, or take orders from a man one hated. If I had had a career of that in the army, it now was done—there was nothing left in the first twenty-four years of my life to write about; one way or another, my life seemed to have been mined and melted into the long reaches of the book. And so I was prominent and empty, and I had to begin life again.*[1]

On this and other occasions, Mailer identifies a new, provisional identity that allegedly has little relation to the person he used to be. As we shall see in *The Armies of the Night*, Mailer more specifically repudiates his past—his childhood and Jewish heritage—and articulates a transcendent or existential self that is nominally redefined in the context of new experiences. While Mailer continued to write novels in the following decades—among them, *Barbary Shore* (1951) and *Why Are We in Viet-*

nam? (1967)—he revealed, as did some of the Beat writers of the 1950s, an all-encompassing pursuit of experience that would lead him into a variety of social, political, and literary arenas. Mailer was, for example, one of the founding members of *The Village Voice*, and in 1959 he published *Advertisements for Myself*, a personal and confessional work that anticipated the personal journalism (New Journalism) of the 1960s and identified a Maileresque desire to "settle for nothing less than making a revolution in the consciousness of our time."[2] In 1969 Mailer pursued a slightly more modest ambition when he ran for mayor of New York. (He finished fourth in a field of five.) Mailer also played a small part as architect Stanford White in the critically acclaimed *Ragtime* (1981). Several years later he directed his first feature length film, *Tough Guys Don't Dance*, an existential detective story similar in plot and characterization to his controversial and serialized novel *An American Dream* (1965). Prior to these cinematic (ad)ventures, Mailer produced, wrote, and acted in three experimental films: *Wild 90*, *Beyond the Law*, and *Maidstone*. In addition, Mailer has written approximately a dozen books of nonfiction—among them, *Miami and the Siege of Chicago* (1968), *Of a Fire on the Moon* (1970), *St. George and the Godfather* (1972), *The Fight* (1974), Pulitzer Prize winning *The Executioner's Song* (1979), and *The Armies of the Night* (1968), winner of both the Pulitzer Prize and National Book Award. The publication of *Armies* helped resuscitate Mailer's literary reputation, much as the critical and popular success of *In Cold Blood* (1965) had boosted Truman Capote's faltering career three years earlier.

Though Mailer has written about a variety of subjects, politics and boxing to name just two, most all of his nonfiction writing addresses what it means to be a representative or mythic American figure: a politician (Kennedy, Nixon), a celebrity/actress (Marilyn Monroe), a writer (Hemingway/Mailer), or other emblematic types. "Like Emerson," John Hollowell explains, Mailer feels that to understand an era or an event you need "to study its representative men [and women]."[3] Mailer shares this interest in representative figures with *The New Yorker* writer John McPhee, another notable but very different literary journalist. Though their ideologies (world views) and journalism practices are radically different, they both define and explore national character by focusing on specific personality types. McPhee idealizes individual selves who share several traditional American values and beliefs, whereas Mailer often identifies representative types—soldiers, Southerners, and military police, for example—who are emblematic of certain aspects of the American experience, character, and psyche.

Mailer may be quick to categorize others and impute personality traits to them, but he also reveals a personal need to preserve, even defend, the sovereignty of the singular self within a culture that encourages us to construct identities, according to Christopher Lasch, "out of materials furnished by advertising and mass culture, themes of popular film and fiction, and fragments torn from a vast range of cultural traditions, all of them equally contemporaneous to the contemporary mind."[4] While at times Mailer indeed "seeks contamination" amidst this accumulation of cultural detritus by "adopting the roles, the styles, the sounds that will give him the measure of what it's like to be alive in this country,"[5] throughout *The Armies of the Night* he repeatedly acknowledges the difficulty of articulating an acceptable identity within social contexts that confer and even bestow an identity. In spite or perhaps because of these external pressures, Mailer constructs a self-centered universe by appropriating public occasions and transforming them into symbolic stages on which he can dramatize the self as an existential performer. Though these theatrical displays of ego often evoke criticism even from some of Mailer's most ardent admirers, they often represent significant autobiographical and ritual moments that allow him to cultivate a combative personality and affirm a masculine identity based on competitive and even aggressive encounters with public officials and representative cultural figures as well as social peers and friends.

As in a number of other works of literary journalism—Hunter S. Thompson's *Fear and Loathing: On the Campaign Trail '72*, Tom Wolfe's *The Right Stuff*, and Michael Herr's *Dispatches*—Mailer repeatedly criticizes conventional journalism and identifies representatives from the media as some of his principal adversaries. *The Armies of the Night* begins, in fact, with a passage from *Time* magazine that recounts the series of speeches given by Mailer, Robert Lowell, Paul Goodman, and Dwight Macdonald at the Ambassador Theater in Washington, D.C. on the night before the march on the Pentagon. The unidentified *Time* reporter writes that Mailer performed an "unscheduled scatological solo" while he slurped bourbon from a coffee mug and "staggered about the stage—which he had commandeered by threatening to beat up the previous M.C."[6] Mailer follows the article with a one-sentence paragraph: "Now we may leave *Time* in order to find out what happened."[7] This comment and the ironically chosen chapter title, "Pen Pals," underscore Mailer's longstanding adversarial relationshp with the press and other media. John Hollowell points out that "clearly Mailer intends *Armies* as an antidote to the inevitable distortions of the traditional press. . . . Mailer's book is an explicit attack on the 'objectivity' and impersonality of the conventional media."[8] In this and other textual moments Mailer raises questions about mass communication and the relationship between media images and their corresponding reality, particularly in regard to how the press creates and disseminates prepackaged images of celebrities and public figures. The construction of a socially acceptable public identity, Mailer suggests throughout *Armies*, is based on the struggle between the individual (ego) and the shaping powers of the various media. Mailer explains that "during the day . . . newspapermen and other assorted bravos of the media and the literary world would carve ugly pictures on the living tomb of his legend. Of necessity, part of" his "remaining funds of sensitivity went right into the war of supporting his image and working for it."[9] Though Mailer indicates that the press and "other bravos of the media and literary world" both defame his character and define a familiar (and negative) public image, he successfully uses the media as an extension of his ego and as a means to create a more acceptable—or at least chosen—public identity.

Like Hunter S. Thompson, Mailer cultivates an aggressive persona and suggests that it is in part fostered as a response to misrepresentation and slipshod reporting. Mailer's struggle for self-definition is based in part on the struggle to control language—the ability to articulate a self in words in a mass-mediated environment that easily absorbs all idiosyncratic and alternative voices and presentations of self and transforms them into commodities for public consumption. In *Of a Fire on the Moon*, *Miami and the Siege of Chicago*, *The Executioner's Song*, and, in particular, *The Armies of the Night*, Mailer employs a number of provisional voices and personae—among them, "the reporter," "Aquarius," "revolutionary-for-a-weekend," "the beast"—which identify and attempt to counter his distrust of organizational conformity and consensus. The plurality of Mailer's address, moreover, is often controlled, as it is in the writing of Wolfe, by an authorial voice that assumes that it "can be free of its inevitable interactions with other social voices."[10]

Richard Poirier points out that Mailer "is the stout literary contender for the English language, in competition not simply with others . . . but with anything—transistors, newspapers, tapes, the sound of helicopters, all the media—that presumes to represent reality."[11] If Tom Wolfe understands contemporary experience as a form of tacit and at times calculated game-playing between social players, Mailer interprets social interaction in terms of a metaphorical and at times actual "battle," "fight," or "war." In both *The Armies of the Night* and *Of a Fire on the Moon* it would be inappropriate, as Chris Anderson explains, to see Mailer's spectator role as passive. As is often the case throughout Mailer's writing, the "dominant mood for Mailer is combat."[12] This combative stance is often achieved by separating himself from the subjects he describes and regularly identifying this opposition. In *Of a Fire on the Moon*, for example, Mailer perceives press conferences with the astronauts as a kind of battle in which he and other journalists struggle with and press the astronauts to say something meaningful about going into space.[13] *The Armies of the Night* is replete with similar images and language, as the following references reveal: "he [Robert Lowell] indisputably won the first round";[14] "going to battle";[15] "four battling sweet wives";[16] and "the effect was equal to walloping a roundhouse right into the heart of an English boxer."[17] These and other key phrases and images, prevalent throughout *The Armies of the Night*, identify the confrontational dimension of the march (on the Pentagon), establish appropriate (metaphorical) terms for discussing the political and social realities of the late 1960s, and specify a masculine rhetoric that coincides with, and often characterizes, personal and symbolic encounters based on (potential) conflict rather than cooperation and negotiation. More generally, Mailer's use of metaphor, Barbara Lounsberry explains, "involves a kind of journey" which "takes his reader repeatedly on trips, often (for this is the very nature of metaphor) against their will." The use of metaphor, in other words, is a "coercive" act.[18] While metaphors enlarge our understanding of a subject, or subjects, they are also, in Mailer's re-imagined world, rhetorical and stylistic emblems that both reveal and help define the combative and at times aggressive persona we see in the following example.

When Mailer and other protestors cross a bridge on their way to the Pentagon, a boy gets upset when the marchers come to a temporary halt: " 'Why don't we move? Why don't we just push ahead?' " he asks. Mailer intuits that something is wrong, and even wonders if "provocateurs" were sent "to start violence within the ranks on the bridge."[19] Mailer is annoyed by the boy's aggressiveness and is ready to fight if necessary. He explains, however, that "he would of course not throw the first punch, not ever! That would be just what he would need for his reputation. To throw the punch which started the rumble which wrecked the March on the Pentagon! And every camera in town to pick up the action."[20] Mailer, of course, intentionally overstates his influence on the outcome of the march. He acknowledges that he is indeed a prisoner of his ego; that moments of self-aggrandizement either distort his perceptions of events or encourage behavior that is not always in his best interest, particularly when TV cameras are present.

Regardless of the young man's intentions, Mailer's contentious spirit represents, moreover, part of his own personality, which he at once covets but finds increasingly difficult to maintain. The potential conflict with the alleged "provocateurs" is emblematic of the identity struggle occurring within Mailer himself. On more than one occasion the forty-four-year-old Mailer indicates that he "had been suffering more and more in the past few years from the private conviction that he was getting a little soft . . . around the edges."[21] He explains that "he could feel himself becoming more and more of a modest man . . . and he hated this because modesty was an old family relative, he had been born to a modest family, had been a modest boy, a modest young man, and he hated that, he loved the pride and the arrogance and the confidence . . . he had acquired over the years."[22] The combative spirit that so frequently characterizes his interaction with others animates moments of personal introspection and self-definition. These private convictions and worries are often dramatized in symbolic moments throughout *The Armies of the Night.*

One of the most revealing incidents occurs shortly after Mailer is arrested. He is placed in an army truck with several other demonstrators, one of whom is a younger man with blond hair and a Nazi armband on his shirt sleeve. Shortly after Mailer and the Nazi are involved in a staring contest—the kind of contest Mailer seldom loses. When Mailer prevails the Nazi quickly counters with:

> "You Jew bastard. . . . Dirty Jew with Kinky hair."
> "You filthy Kraut," Mailer responds.
> "Dirty Jew."
> "Kraut Pig."[23]

The verbal sparring continues until a U.S. marshal jumps in the truck and tells them to be quiet. The marshal eventually slams the butt of his club into the Nazi's collarbone and bounces him several times against the wall of the truck. Then the truck begins to move, and everybody appears calmer. Silent. Mailer explains that "some small storm of hysteria seemed to have worked itself out of the van."[24] Though Mailer seldom provokes such encounters, he suggests that the Nazi's presence is an encroachment on his personal, ideological, and physical space. He seeks to control this territory by symbolically possessing the Nazi's soul in a staring contest and maximizing the force, or energy, immanent in such exchanges. The Nazi challenges Mailer's minor victory by identifying his adversary with his own chosen terms, 'dirty Jew' and 'Jew bastard.' While the battle of male wills is never resolved, the outcome of the encounter is less important than Mailer's personal struggle.

On the one hand, it is not only that Mailer refuses to be categorized and negatively defined by the Nazi; he is also reminded about an aspect of self he seemingly wishes to repudiate, as the following passage suggests. Mailer explains that the "last remaining speck of the one personality he found absolutely insupportable" was "the nice Jewish boy from Brooklyn."[25] While this and other autobiographical moments are often fraught with seemingly contradictory messages, or at least multi-layered ones, Mailer makes no attempt to construct, as does John McPhee, a rational, coherent self based on an immutable model of identity. Identity formation is an ongoing struggle, neither the unfolding of an indisputable and unescapable nature (or essence) nor merely the affirmation of a socially determined and acceptable public identity. Mailer attempts to fashion an original, existential self—and not always successfully—which transcends family, religion, even biology. Just as "Mailer wishes to speak in a language that celebrates incompletion,"[26] as Malini Johar Schueller points out, he also articulates a self through an array of plural voices and personae that identify a similar lack of completion in his understanding of personal identity.

Mailer's interaction with the Nazi is also, of course, a test of courage, a challenge that allows him to dismiss temporarily both the "modest man" and the "nice Jewish boy from Brooklyn" while he affirms a generic male identity based on a ritual display of physical prowess. Barry Leeds points out that "the most striking thing about Mailer's protagonist is a new sense of modesty and personal limitation. He is often frightened and weak, uncertain of how he will react in the face of moral confrontation or physical danger."[27] While there is indeed a "new sense of modesty," a recognition of "personal limitation," it contributes to, or is at least offset by, an obsession with physical bravery, which may temporarily allay insecurities and fears while it prohibits, it would seem, the possibility of real growth or change. Mailer maintains that he "never had a particular age—he carried different ages within him like different models of his experience: parts of him were eighty-one years old, fifty-seven, forty-eight, thirty-six, nineteen, et cetera, et cetera."[28] Yet, he reveals an implicit and real concern about middle age (growing older) that necessitates that he reclaim a specific age, or model of self, based on conventionally masculine ideas—strength, physical power, even reckless courage—often associated with youth or adolescence. Andrew Gordon points out that the conflict in the book "is as much internal as it is external; it is not simply Mailer vs. the Pentagon, but Mailer vs. Mailer," "the rite of passage of a middle-aged man who is uncertain of his manhood and confused about his identity."[29]

A similar encounter occurs in *Miami and the Siege of Chicago*. Near the end of the Democratic convention in Chicago when Mailer feels ambivalent about his modest role as journalistic observer—at one point he watches the action (violence) in the street from the safety of his nineteenth-floor hotel room—he feels compelled, gratuitously it seems, to precipitate a fight. Bolstered by a measurable amount of alcohol, a minor schuffle occurs with soldiers when Mailer disobeys a National Guard Officer's request to step back from a military jeep, which the author claims, asserting the role of pugnacious journalist, that he has a right to describe. (Mailer wrote the article for *Harper's Magazine*.) Shortly after this incident is resolved, Mailer has another brief but more serious altercation with an alleged convention delegate who he identifies—with a paranoia almost equal to Hunter S. Thompson's—as a possible "police provocateur." Mailer gets punched in the eye—somewhat unexpectedly—but before he can attack his assailant two police officers restrain his advances. At that point, Mailer's imagination takes over; he speculates that the police were going to "gang [fight] him on this floor out of the violent creativity of their paranoia."[30] Mailer realizes then

> that he was not really afraid, he did not feel weak—scared, he felt, and very awake, but he was ready, he was going to try to do his best when they started to work. He did not feel in a jelly or a bath—he felt as electric and crazy as the cops. The fact that he had this sentiment now, that he was ready to fight, made him feel close to some presence with a beatific grace (for he felt it, he felt with this readiness to fight as if the air were beautiful where it was near him) and that left him happy, happier than he had been any moment since he had heard the awful cry of the wounded pig in his throat at the news Bobby Kennedy was shot.[31]

Mailer is brought before Commander Lyons and tells him that he does not want to be arrested. After several minutes of friendly conversation—and after Mailer's reputation is discussed—the officers let him go to meet his friends. Mailer joins Pete Hamill and Doug Kiker—his drinking buddies—and they head over to Hugh Hefner's Playboy mansion for a few more drinks. As the concluding portion of this passage suggests, Mailer's physical confrontation is ostensibly salutary and redemptive, a way of confronting and purging an array of feelings—fear, ambivalence, loss—that were percolating inside him throughout his coverage of the convention. Mailer's deliverance and self-awareness also invoke the myth of regeneration through violence and paradoxically identify a romantic sense of well-being based on risk and the possibility of physical injury. The romanticizing of risk, danger, and physical confrontation, particularly as they relate to the construction and affirmation of a generic male (masculine) identity, are central, if implicit, concerns—often unexplored concerns—in several other significant works of literary journalism: Michael Herr's *Dispatches*, Tom Wolfe's *The Right Stuff*, George Plimpton's *Shadow Box* and *Paper Lion*, and Joe McGinniss' *Fatal Vision*, *Blind Faith*, and *Cruel Doubt*.

Of all these writers, Mailer is, of course, the one most often criticized for his preoccupation with "masculine" subject matter and his overt displays of aggressive behavior. I would argue, however, that this annoying concern is also one of the endearing qualities of Mailer's writing, and it is inextricably tied to his belief that taking risks is central to (his) life, even if they result in failure, or are possibly accompanied by guilt or shame. One particularly revealing example occurs early in *The Armies of the Night* when Mailer learns from Ed de Grazia (the main lawyer for the mobilization's Legal Defense Committee) that an M.C. has not yet been appointed for the evening of speeches at the Ambassador Theater. Mailer takes advantage of this opportunity, despite that it may result in embarrassment and failure. He tells the reader that he "was already composing his introductory remarks, percolating along on thoughts of subtle annoyance his role as Master of Ceremonies would cause the other speakers."[32] Before Mailer takes the stage, however, he has an overwhelming need to urinate. Afterward, he finds, much to his irritation, that the speeches have started without him—and with de Grazia serving as M.C. Paul Goodman finishes his speech and Mailer informs de Grazia that he is going to assume the role that is rightfully his. Due to an excessive amount of static—a product of American technocracy that competes with Mailer's voice—he chooses to speak directly to his audience. He begins an impromptu speech, sips from a mug of bourbon, and quickly elicits boos from the crowd. One spectator shouts, " 'publicity hound,' " and Mailer responds with a " 'fuck you' " before he continues with his existential monologue. At one point Mailer reveals that he had a problem in the men's room prior to the speech: because he couldn't find the light switch he ended up urinating on the floor. Mailer finally relinquishes the spotlight to Robert Lowell, and later he acknowledges that he "was jealous because he had worked for this audience, and Lowell without effort seemed to have stolen them."[33]

Much like Hunter S. Thompson, Mailer quite consciously subverts the seriousness of certain occasions and strives to incite and annoy others, including readers, by presenting himself in a way that disrupts the commonsense order of events. While Mailer presents himself as the flawed anti-hero—comical, belligerent, ineffectual, and fraught with contradictions—his need to be admired, or at least listened to, is matched only by a querulous propensity to bully and eventually polarize the very audience he wishes to embrace—and be embraced by. Mailer is not unlike the recalcitrant boy who elicits negative attention from others because it is better than no attention at all. While Mailer's general stage behavior seems largely irrelevant to the occasion, by chronicling events in the third person, portraying himself as "your protagonist" or "the Participant," he "succeeds in the writing," as Richard Poirier points out, "by admitting that he failed as a participant."[34] John Hollowell similarly notes that Mailer's use of " 'the Reporter' as the protagonist" in *Miami and the Siege of Chicago* "serves conveniently as a rhetorical strategy for masking Mailer's errors and omissions. Missing the story can be attributed to the human foibles of the Reporter, not to all-knowing, famous novelist Norman Mailer."[35]

This calculated self-distancing also allows Mailer to re-invent the self and cast events in theatrical terms. Regardless of the "protagonist's" original intentions, his allegedly spontaneous (existential) and inappropriate behavior represents one moment in which Mailer articulates a metaphor of self by playing a role—"the beast" or "wild man"—which reinforces the public's perception of him. Mailer may indeed be on the brink of personal discovery, but his retreat into self-parody at once mitigates criticism by anticipating it and largely prohibits a more in-depth exploration of the private person. Mailer seems more concerned with extending the boundaries of his experiences and influence than deepening what he knows about himself, if such a distinction can be made. Moreover, Mailer's behavior here and throughout *The Armies of the Night* identifies his awareness of himself as a consummate role-player. Like Hunter S. Thompson, Mailer seems to live his life in anticipation of its theatrical and narrative worth. While autobiographical writing is based typically on and preceded by the exceptional character and life, Mailer reverses this premise by suggesting that they are in part the result of marketing, opportunism, and manipulation of mass media.

Because Mailer's behavior is a form of calculated expression, rather than unpremeditated action, it might be interpreted as a kind of "street theater," an acknowledgment that public events and occasions, particularly in the light of intense media coverage and audience expectations, constitute a theater of everyday life. Mailer's personal histrionics, moreover, are relevant to how we finally interpret the "meaning" of the demonstration itself. In the second and much shorter section of the work—"The Novel as History: The Battle of the Pentagon"—Mailer provides a more objective and "factual" account of the march. While this legitimates Mailer's claims that he is indeed writing a history, if only a highly impressionistic one, it also allows him to describe more specifically the preparations for the march and the meetings between demonstrators and public officials. As Mailer provides details of the negotiations—for example, where the participants can congregate, what access roads they can use—it becomes increasingly clear that the event is in effect a symbolic cultural drama, or media event, orchestrated and "staged" in a manner similar to the author's own calculated behavior and self-serving display of histrionics. While a writer like John McPhee acknowledges the importance of reconstructing a recognizable physical reality in a world in which knowledge and experiences are increasingly part of a mass-mediated environment, Mailer more readily embraces the provisional and theatrical dimensions of social life in a quickly changing post-industrial culture.

Mailer's moments of self-aggrandizement prophetically anticipated and perhaps helped to create a cultural model—the "performing self"—which would soon be embraced in the late 1960s by both a growing adversarial culture and a society characterized increasingly by displays of self-promotion and often blatant exhibitionism, whether it was fornicating on stage in an off-Broadway play or wearing a see-through blouse. The need to distinguish oneself from the mass of undifferentiated others was in part the result of a changing society that imposed specific burdens on the self—in fact, threatened to obviate the self by bureaucratic cooptation, nuclear destruction, or incorporation in an impersonal economic organization. A society that allegedly endorsed individualism and celebrated the efficacy of personal achievement was, in fact, minimizing autonomy and even interfering, or intruding upon, the private lives of Americans. For Mailer, the "preoccupation with man's diminishing role in a centralized society has been a consistent theme since his first novel."[36] The sovereignty of the self is regularly threatened by the media and an industrial technocracy that permeates our lives and is represented in Mailer's world by such commonplace but symbolically meaningful objects as diaphragms and telephones.

Not surprisingly, the primacy of experience is the principal way Mailer authenticates a self and understands personal and social realities. Mailer tries to create a self-oriented world by positioning himself, whenever possible, at the center of social events and creating a politics of personal witness often predicated on spontaneity and intuition. This is vividly dramatized when Mailer is clustered with other restless demonstrators about fifty yards from a group of military police who are positioned on one side of the Pentagon. Mailer looks at Dwight Macdonald and Robert Lowell and says, " 'Let's go.' " As he makes his charge, Mailer explains that he felt "disembodied from himself, as if indeed he were watching himself in a film where this action was taking place. He could feel the eyes of the people behind the rope watching him, could feel the intensity of their existence as spectators."[37] Mailer eventually passes one line of military police but is wrestled down before he reaches the Pentagon. We might customarily assume that participation in a demonstration or protest would result in the subordination of the self and the affirmation of a collective identity based on shared experience and congruent political beliefs. Mailer, however, refuses to relinquish personal control (of the event) by submerging his identity within a group of anonymous demonstrators, even though his "heroic" gesture results in the arrest that prevents him from playing a more significantly active and symbolic role in the demonstration.

We later learn that Mailer's seemingly spontaneous and perhaps dangerous behavior was recorded by a group of documentary filmmakers. In withholding this information from the reader, Mailer acknowledges the fictive nature of his enterprise by preserving—rather, creating—the drama of his self-conscious performance. This seems to validate Mailer's literary powers while it raises questions about his political intentions. But Mailer is quite aware, as the previous passage underscores, that the march on the Pentagon is both a staged performance and a symbolic event. The success of the march depends greatly on anticipated media coverage. Journalists characteristically identify luminaries within the mass of demonstrators and later feature them in print or on TV. Before the march commences, Mailer even ironically observes that he, Lowell, and Macdonald "were requested to get up in the front row [of demonstrators], where the notables were to lead the March, a row obviously to be consecrated for the mass media."[38] Mailer adds, three pages later, that if "his head was to be busted this day," let this symbolic moment be seen by "the eyes of America's TV viewers tonight."[39] Mailer acknowledges that he is playing, for himself and for the media, the role of "revolutionary-for-a-weekend." As a cultural performer and public figure Mailer is quite conscious of how he positions and perceives himself in relation to political and social events. Unlike most other literary journalists, Mailer seems able to participate physically in an event while he simultaneously retains an element of detachment. When Mailer explains that "he could feel the eyes of the people behind the ropes watching him, could feel the intensity of their existence as spectators," he is able to objectify his experience in writing through third-person narration and describe himself as others—bystanders—might perceive him. Mailer not only affirms an imperial self but in effect co-opts the entire event by casting other participants in the role of witnesses who validate his existential performance.

In *Miami and the Siege of Chicago*, Mailer has a similar opportunity to play "revolutionary-for-a-weekend." The playful grandstanding in *The Armies of the Night*, however, is eschewed in favor of a more detached journalistic position. This is most dramatically illustrated when Mailer is situated in his hotel room—nineteen floors up, as I noted earlier—while the police below are chasing and clubing demonstrators. Mailer's physical separation is accepted, not surprisingly, with some reservation: he worries about his dwindling courage, feels chagrin when three of his friends—William Burroughs, Jean Genet, and Allen Ginsberg—participate in a demonstration he avoids. Mailer concludes that "one could protest with one's body, one could be tear-gassed . . . and one could take a crack on the head with a policeman's stick, or a going-over by plainclothesmen" but "the reporter had an aversion to this."[40] Moreover, as a participant Mailer would likely be just another anonymous body in the large group of demonstrators. His elevated position allows him to establish authorial omniscience and reconstruct the event from a panoramic point of view. Individual motivations and actions are yoked to Mailer's metaphorical assessment of the scene as a "murderous" paradigm of the Vietnam War, a symbolic interpretation of an event that validates Mailer's interpretive and descriptive powers while it identifies his position of aesthetic and moral privilege.

While Mailer can often in effect "steal the show," as these examples illustrate, there are other occasions when he is noticeably upset when he is not at the center of events. On the morning after the Ambassador Theater and prior to the march, for example, Mailer feels not only hungover but excluded from a group of demonstrators who have gathered in the basement of a Reformation church to prepare for the day's events. Mailer is offended that he is not asked to speak. And when he sees Dwight Macdonald and Robert Lowell conversing in an open area at the front of the room, only ten feet away, he wonders "whether it would be worse to believe they had chosen not to recognize him, or that he was merely sufficiently paranoid to assume such a decision."[41] Mailer adds that

> what aggravated this small matter was the generally cool treatment he was receiving, since no one of the two hundred or more people sitting and standing about had come up to introduce themselves and mention that they liked his work or wished to say hello, an occurrence normally so common and so conventionally annoying to a score of the most established American authors that they feel unmanned when it fails to occur.[42]

Mailer's desire to be recognized and at the center of events is problematic for the author as well as the reader. Mailer, of course, wants to be considered a successful, if not great, American writer; he wants to make sure, Richard Poirier points out, "that he will be read with care bordering on fear, with expectation bordering on shame."[43] With Mailer's considerable talent, these are certainly not unrealistic expectations. But his desire for literary success is also freighted with an implicit narcissism centered on a regressive, even infantile need to be admired by others and an inability, as we shall see later, to grant them an autonomous existence outside his own. While Mailer can accept that Robert Lowell is perhaps America's greatest living poet (in 1967), he nonetheless "felt hot anger at how Lowell was loved and he was not."[44] Part of Mailer's need to see this aggrandized self reflected in the adulation of others may grow out of a sense that, regardless of his literary success, he will invariably be excluded from certain centers of power and arenas of American life. This is suggested in *The Armies of the Night* when Mailer observes that when Lowell was "chatting with old friends farther up the line . . . he looked for the moment like one Harvard dean talking to another, that same genteel confidential gracious hunch of the shoulder toward each other. No dean at Harvard had ever talked to *him* that way, Mailer now decided bitterly."[45] Mailer's depiction of the genteel Lowell, embodiment of "that old-fashioned Wasp integrity," identifies the author's marginal status and reveals his desire to be a more fully integrated part of American life. Mailer's acknowledged bitterness may reveal a personal resentment based on the alienation experienced by cultural outsiders, specifically, some Jewish-Americans. Yet, paradoxically, Lowell's dignified gentility represents much of what Mailer "the beast" abhors: "everything principled and austere in the American character."[46] Mailer would in all likelihood spurn any form of social membership that challenges the sanctity of the singular self.

Mailer may in some senses be excluded from certain centers of power, but he can symbolically control these moments by constructing a self-governed literary world and "appropriating through metaphors [or writing] any experience that threatens to remain independent of him."[47] This is evident, for example, when Mailer is placed in an army truck and later in jail. He explains that because he is a "prisoner of his own egotism, some large vital part of the March had ended for him with his own arrest. He was poor material for a general indeed if he had no sense of the major combat twenty miles away."[48] Mailer's incarceration is exacerbated by the fact that he is not only a prisoner of the state but a captive of admirers and potential sycophants who breach his personal space. One grips Mailer's arm and says: " 'We got to talk.' " " 'When the time comes, buddy,' " Mailer replies, as he throws off his arm.[49] Mailer then explains that to survive in prison he had to "imprison" his "own best instincts" and "avoid anything which looked like action"[50]—particularly fighting. In such an environment, Mailer suggests, it is necessary to deny aspects of the self in order to preserve it. Prison life in effect strips inmates of their individuality; preservation of self is increasingly determined by denial and self-control. Mailer's principal means of empowerment is the assertion of human consciousness. He transcends the physical and psychological barriers of his confinement by repossessing and projecting a meaning onto the larger world he can no longer influence or control by action or physical prowess. Nowhere is this more evident than when Mailer is first incarcerated in an army truck that will eventually take him and other demonstrators to jail. He observes that

> the gang of Marshals now studied outside the bus were enough to firm up any fading loyalty to his own cause: they had the kind of faces which belong to the bad guys in a Western. Some were fat, some were too thin, but nearly all seemed to have those subtle anomalies of the body which come often to men from small towns who have inherited strong features, but end up, by their own measure, in failure. Some would have powerful chests, but abrupt paunches, the skinny ones would have a knob in the shoulder, or a hitch in their gait, their foreheads would have odd cleaving wrinkles, so that one man might look as if an ax had struck him between the eyes, another paid tithe to ten parallel deep lines rising in ridges above his eye brows. The faces of all too many had a low cunning mixed with a stroke of rectitude: if the mouth was slack, the nose was straight and severe; should the lips be tight, the nostrils showed an outsize greed. . . . These Marshals had the dead eye and sour cigar, that sly shuffle of propriety and rut which so often comes out in a small-town sheriff as patriotism and the sweet stink of a crooked dollar.[51]

Like Tom Wolfe, Mailer rarely individualizes characters by probing their emotional and psychological makeup. In this and other instances, he observes his subjects from a physical and symbolic distance and interprets their physical features and gestures as representative cultural types. While this and other characterizations (or portraits) are, as John Hellmann observes, "completely intuitive, obviously stereotyped, and no doubt to some degree unfair,"[52] they represent "the act of a mind reaching out to the world in order to *create* meaning, a meaning which is both dynamic and tentative, for it is a construct of active interplay between interior consciousness and external fact."[53] Mailer, in other words, projects metaphorical meaning onto external objects and people, whereas a writer like John McPhee attempts to construct a realistic world populated with recognizable and more fully-rounded characters. Mailer reveals an ability to penetrate, like a phrenologist, the psychic contours of a subject's character by attending to specific physical and symbolic features. On the one hand Mailer seems to escape accusations of solipsism by transforming personal observations into resonant, multi-layered statements about American life, but he paradoxically affirms a dimension of social life only to find his "solitude" as a cultural observer—in this case, prisoner—intensified. Mailer's attempts to identify and explore national character, if only in metaphorical terms, manifest themselves "only in the private dialogues of the mind with itself."[54] At times, the material world vitiates, as it does in the writings of Joan Didion and Tom Wolfe, because Mailer insists on interpreting reality on his narrow and metaphorical terms.

Mailer's understanding of Americans and American life is rooted in the ideology of the 1950s and is both a critique and product of the kind of cultural criticisms produced in this decade. The cultural critics of the 1950s identified individuals as role-players and system's people who were defined by institutional dictates and controlled by an Orwellian web of manipulators and hidden persuaders. In national character and myth and symbol studies, as well as in works of sociology—among them, Henry Nash Smith's *Virgin Land* (1950), R.W.B. Lewis' *The American Adam*, John Ward's *Andrew Jackson, Symbol for an Age* (1955), William Whyte's *The Organization Man* (1956), and Vance Packard's *The Hidden Persuaders* (1957)—the emphasis on organic holism and the identification of specific character types presume a uniform cultural life and a consensus of anonymous people who respond to, or are defined by, a historically determined model of identity. Mailer's understanding of contemporary American life is often based on a similar attempt to explain national character: what it means to be an American, or a certain kind of American. While Mailer may indeed condemn American totalitarianism—"the machine" that grinds out "mass man"—he also succumbs to an autocratic impulse by homogenizing some of his characters as types and/or refusing to grant them identities outside of his shaping influence.

Mailer's depiction of others is always, however, a way of understanding and enlarging the boundaries of the self. While Mailer may neither understand the individual personalities of his subjects nor fully comprehend the implications of the march on the Pentagon, *The Armies of the Night* seems, according to Andrew Gordon, "the inevitable culmination of Mailer's long search for a way of dealing with [and understanding] himself in print."[55] Robert Merrill explains that "Mailer's divided self" and battling personalities achieve "at least temporary wholeness during the March on the Pentagon." If part I (of Book One) reveals Mailer's alleged apathy, parts II and III chronicle his growing involvement and full-fledged commitment to this now historical and symbolic event.[56] Mailer's participation might more generally be understood as a conversion experience—"a rite of purification" to use Merrill's terms—that culminates in his release from prison and in a renewed understanding of himself. Mailer explains that "standing on the grass, he felt one suspicion of a whole man closer to that freedom from dread which occupied the inner drama of his years, yes, one image closer than when he had come to Washington four days ago. The sum of what he had done that he considered good outweighed the dull sum of his omissions these same four days."[57] As this and other comments suggest, Mailer's exploration of self is an ongoing spiritual (existential) quest (process) in which his identity is bound and transformed by a view of human nature that interprets individuals as a complex set of motivations and desires. While the writings of McGinniss, Didion, Thompson, and other literary journalists are undeniably personal and at times autobiographical, Mailer's *The Armies of the Night* most vividly reveals the ambiguous tensions and impulses embedded in autobiographical writing. As in most other revealing works of life-writing, the need to rationalize, apologize for, and even repress dimensions of self-exploration is perhaps only superseded by a similar and seemingly paradoxical desire to uncover, explore, and know the inscrutable self.

8

Conclusion: The Therapeutic and "Hidden" Selves

At the end of chapter 6, I note that Hunter S. Thompson's journalism pieces often conclude with the author's self-imposed exile (from society). This real and metaphorical escape to his Woody Creek home coincided with the counterculture's rural retreat at the decade's end and prefigured the therapeutic quest for selfhood that followed in the 1970s. These cultural trends corresponded with two distinct and at times overlapping ways in which literary journalists conceptualized and presented the self through the 1970s and into the 1980s. Instead of focusing on the urban milieu as the setting and subject of their works, which characterized much of the New Journalism of the 1960s, many literary journalists and nonfiction writers—among them, Mark Kramer, Wendell Berry, Carol Bly, Jane Kramer, and, of course, John McPhee—revealed an increased interest in rural, regional, ecological, environmental, and historical subject matter. In turn they presented a more modulated, even concealed self in which the journalist was removed from the center of action and personal concerns were often revealed in only the most indirect ways. Other literary journalists, however, conceptualized a therapeutic and an examined self, as I noted in chapter 3, that coincided with the therapeutic sensibility of the 1970s and is represented by selected writings from Joan Didion's *The White Album* (1979), Sara Davidson's *Real Property* (1981), and Nora Ephron's *Crazy Salad* (1975).

The interest in mental well-being is perhaps most vividly illustrated in Joe McGinniss' *Heroes* (1976), Robert Pirsig's *Zen and the Art of Motorcycle Maintenance* (1974), John Gregory Dunne's *Vegas* (1974), and Peter

Matthiessen's *The Snow Leopard* (1978). These four writers identify the traditionally masculine prerogative of travel and affirm the virtues of individualism and self-determination while simultaneously acknowledging that escape from confining personal and social circumstances is in itself a therapeutic ideal. In *Vegas*, for example, author John Gregory Dunne describes how he is preoccupied with his mortality and unable to work (write). After experiencing a nervous breakdown, he goes to Las Vegas and later explains that there is a therapeutic dimension to reporting that allows the journalist to anesthetize his personal problems while he explores the lives of others. He acknowledges that he has found a subject that will provide "salvation" with little commitment. Dunne soon discovers, however, that Vegas is in fact a refraction of his own misery and that the three principal characters—a prostitute, a private detective, and a lounge comic—mirror his own troubled life and identify his motives for reporting. His capacity for voyeurism, for invading and exposing the lives of others, allows him to minimize "psychic responsibility" and repudiate all commitments while he works through his problems by writing about others. He finally returns home, at the end of the book, presumably a healed or a healthier person. Pirsig's *Zen and the Art of Motorcycle Maintenance* represents a more sustained effort to explore the world of the mentally unstable self. Pirsig, his son, and two friends cross America on motorcycles. The trip is a philosophical and psychological journey, complemented by imaginative forays into the author's past. We discover that Pirsig was once institutionalized for insanity. In order to achieve a harmonious and integrated self, Pirsig resurrects and exorcises his identity from the past, which he identifies as Phaedrus, and reconceptualizes his relation to a society that dichotomizes experience into classical (rational) and romantic (emotional) modes of understanding. Peter Matthiessen redefines his relation to the world in a similar way when he enters the mystical world of Zen. The death of his wife and preoccupation with mortality prompt Matthiessen to make a pilrimage to the Crystal Mountain (in the Himalayan range) to find the semi-mythical snow leopard. Though Matthiessen delights in the details of everyday life and nominally accepts the impermanence of each moment—including the death of his wife—his journey provides no real answers beyond mere acceptance. Despite moments of brilliant description, *The Snow Leopard* is a book about running away from problems, like both *Vegas* and *Heroes*, and then cloaking them in the trappings of Oriental religion. Matthiessen tries to capture the immediacy of the moment by writing in the present tense and using the journal form, but to communicate the Zen experience is, paradoxically, to lose it.

With the possible exception of Pirsig, Matthiessen and the others never fully repossess an old or ratify a changed self. In fact, their journeys are more often than not mere excursions in which the hopeful expectations and freedom of travel take the place of more systematic examinations of the emotional self. Moreover, while Dunne and McGinniss ostensibly explore and reveal themselves by talking about others, they provide neither an adequate collective (social) identity nor a satisfactory introspective version of self. In his discussion of contemporary memoir, Francis Russell Hart suggests that contemporary personal recollections of history and social events cannot accommodate (or have not accommodated) truly private motives; yet opting for a collective identity only results in feelings of self-alienation.[1] The texts I discuss here represent, similarly, neither personal acts of repossessing a public world nor a detailed examination of a private, inner life. To a greater or lesser degree, neither Matthiessen, Dunne, Pirsig, nor McGinniss are willing to make full public records of their private lives, and they refuse to compromise even their fragile egos and individuality by defining a self in relation to a larger group or collective.

In three other popular travel pieces of the early 1980s—Jonathan Raban's *Old Glory: An American Voyage* (1981), William Least Heat Moon's *Blue Highways: A Journey into America* (1982), and Joe McGinniss' *Going to Extremes* (1980)—the authors acknowledge, as did Matthiessen and Dunne, that their personal and undefined journeys allow them to escape debilitating or confining social circumstances. As the following comments reveal, these writers invoke the American myth that it is still possible to eschew social responsibilities and commitments and reaffirm the primacy of the singular (male) self on the open road or highway. McGinniss, for example, spent the two previous years "cooped up inside a stuffy little room" working on a book (*Heroes*) "that had turned out to be mostly about the inside of" his "head." He "was hungry for something different: something big, something fresh, something new. Like Alaska."[2] Raban indicates, similarly, that he "had gone stale and dry" living in London and "run out of whatever peculiar reserves of moral capital" are needed for life in the city. Like Dunne, he found himself unable to write, and the tranquilizers were no longer working.[3] So, like Huck Finn before him, he begins his serendipitous odyssey down the great Mississippi in a sixteen-foot boat. When Least Heat Moon finds out that his teaching appointment has been canceled and that his wife, whom he has been separated from for nine months, is seeing a friend named "Rick or Dick or Chick," he decides that "a man who couldn't make things go right could at least go."[4] And on the following day, Least Heat Moon begins his 13,000 mile journey across the United States, a journey that takes him into and out of forty-eight states in a nine-month period.

Though all three writers confess to personal problems, their journalistic occasions—which might provide opportunities to explore the self—are attempts to transcend or escape self-examination by making a more general investigation of American life, as the subtitles to *Blue Highways: A Journey into America* and *Old Glory: An American Voyage* suggest. Raban, McGinniss, and Least Heat Moon intend to capture a disappearing America—the dying river-town culture of the Mississippi, the closing frontier in Alaska, and vanishing rural and small-town communities—through an examination of the particular and commonplace. Their seemingly inadvertent predilection for wandering, however, prevents them from fully achieving their objectives. Raban, for example, begins with no itinerary in mind: "I would try," he explains, "to be as much like a piece of human driftwood as I could manage."[5] When he leaves a woman behind he meets on his journey, Raban acknowledges that she is "right to tag me as a runner-away. . . . On my river trip, I thought, I am doing only what I have always been doing: keeping the sky up by keeping on the run."[6] Similarly, Least Heat Moon takes us in and out of an entire state in little more than a page.

These serendipitous journeys affirm the innumerable virtues of spontaneity, adventure, and anarchic freedom, but the solitary travels—and travails—of these wanderers also reveal their alienation and lack of personal direction. Their inability to remain rooted for even the briefest time, moreover, undermines their purported interest in local color writing and prevents them from fully recreating a sense of place in their nonfictional worlds. In order to be closer to their subjects, Least Heat Moon travels the blue highways (back roads), instead of the interstates, and Raban negotiates the river in a small craft. Yet they both inadvertently treat travel as a form of tourism. While the journey narrative has often represented progress, expansionism, intellectual and moral enlightenment, as well as the quest for meaning itself, at the end of their trips neither Raban nor Least Heat Moon seem sure of what their experiences meant to them. Whereas Hunter S. Thompson concludes his journalism assignments by self-consciously treating his story as a kind of meta- or anti-quest that defies closure and, finally, understanding itself, Raban can only tell the reader that "I had a one-dollar Woolworth's compass; I wanted to get just lost enough to know that I'd found an ending."[7] Least Heat Moon concludes in a similar roundabout manner: "In a season on the blue roads, what had I accomplished? I hadn't sailed the Atlantic in a washtub, or crossed the Gobi by goat cart, or bicycled to Cape Horn. In my own country, I had gone out, had met, had shared. I had stood witness."[8] He adds, several pages later, that

> the circle almost complete, the truck ran the road like the old horse that knows the way. If the circle had come full turn, I hadn't. I can't say, over the miles, that I had learned what I had wanted to know because I hadn't known what I wanted to know. But I *did* learn what I didn't know I wanted to know.[9]

The journey of search and discovery—about America and about the self—is in part reduced to an ambiguous odyssey of escape, a gender-related (male) phenomenon long central to so much American literature and travel writing. These journeys are articulated by individuals who largely eschew, or are silent about, the private motivations and concerns they pay lip service to at the onset of their journeys. What nominally begins as an attempt to redefine a therapeutic self and reclaim the particulars of contemporary American experience in the literary nonfiction of the early 1980s ends, paradoxically, in hesitancy and authorial silence.

The popular works of Raban, McGinniss, and Least Heat Moon do reveal, however, a more general interest in rural life, regionalism, ecology, and conservation. These subjects are a central concern in a wide range of autobiographical writings and works of literary nonfiction authored through the middle 1970s and into the 1980s: Annie Dillard's *Pilgrim at Tinker Creek* (1974); McPhee's *Encounters with the Archdruid* (1971), *The Survival of the Bark Canoe* (1975), and *The Control of Nature* (1989); Jane Kramer's *The Last Cowboy* (1977); Wendell Berry's *The Unsettling of America* (1977); Carol Bly's *Letters from the Country* (1981); Alec Wilkinson's *Moonshine: A Life in Pursuit of White Liquor* (1985), and, among others, Gretel Ehrlich's *The Solace of Open Spaces* (1985). Richard Rhodes, winner of the 1987 National Book Award for *The Making of the Atomic Bomb*, offers a contemporary and historical profile of the American heartland in *The Inland Ground: An Evocation of the American Middle West* (1970). Jane Kramer examines the life of Henry Blanton, a struggling ranch hand who lives in the panhandle of Texas. And in *Three Farms* (1981) Mark Kramer (no relation to Jane Kramer) discusses the geographical and historical development of a New England dairy farm, an Iowa hog and corn farm, and a California corporate farm. Most all of these writers minimize displays of literary exhibitionism, which characterizes much of the New Journalism of the 1960s and early 1970s, but demonstrate, nonetheless, a remarkable control of literary craft and technique.

Their commitment to regional, rural, and ecological values, reflected in a reverence for the particular and the commonplace, discourages more ostentatious, even histrionic presentations of the self. These writers typically transcend private preoccupations and subordinate personal identity quests by focusing more specifically on their nonfiction subject matter. The ethical and epistemological assumptions of these works, in fact, are often based on the implicit presupposition that the individual self, or author, is a no greater (or lesser) part of the whole, whether it be the community, region, or natural environment. The social and political imperative of redefining our ideology of consumption and exploitation and creating a more "nurturing" relation to natural environments is revealed in the lack of authorial intrusion and the decentering of the journalistic self as a principal and causal agent in these worlds. This is a central part of Wendell Berry's ecological stewardship, and it is also a central, if implicit, part of McPhee's "The Encircled River," the first section of *Coming into the Country*. As Philip Terrie explains, "The Encircled River" is "a tightly unified inquiry into the connection between one's awareness of mortality and the implications of this for wilderness preservation."[10] Similarly, in *Basin and Range* (1980), one of McPhee's primary goals is to expand our conception of time by placing the finitude of human experience and life within the concept of geologic (or deep) time.

As early as the 1970s, the practice of journalistic restraint and self-effacement was already evident in the works of investigative and muckraking journalists. While a work like Carl Bernstein and Bob Woodward's *All the President's Men* romanticizes investigative reporters and, at the time, helped certify the celebrity status of journalists, the dramaturgical significance of the participatory journalist's performance is redefined in terms of exhaustive legwork and an unimpeachable commitment to the fidelity of factual reporting. Like the literary nonfiction that would later focus on environmental and ecological concerns, Seymour M. Hersh's *My Lai 4: A Report on the Massacre and Its Aftermath* (1970), C.D.B. Bryan's *Friendly Fire* (1976), and other works of investigative journalism focus on "serious" subject matter—in these examples, death—and implicitly identify the problematic notion of an American imperial self in contexts where human lives seem expandable. On these and other journalistic occasions, the articulation of a participatory or more flamboyant journalistic self would be insensitive and inappropriate, undermining the writer's credibility and compromising completely a journalistic contract based in part on our belief in the journalist as a fair, unselfish, and humane individual. In a later work like *Salvador* (1983), Didion was aware, no doubt, of the journalist's problematic relationship to such difficult and potentially inflammatory subject matter. Her commitment to journalistic detachment—she bears witness to the atrocities and death that surround her in

Salvador—is an attempt to redefine, or at least avoid, the colonialist mentality that conceals ethnocentricism, indifference or contempt, even racism behind either the self-serving, at times arrogant posture of the participatory journalist or the veil of nominally objective and omniscient authority.

The presentation of a more modest journalistic self is also evident in some of the most recent writings of the authors discussed throughout this work: Mailer's *The Executioner's Song*, Didion's *Salvador* (1983) and *Miami* (1987), and McGinniss' *Fatal Vision* (1983), *Blind Faith* (1988), and *Cruel Doubt* (1991). These writers construct personally meaningful and metaphorical worlds in which the self is decentered and relegated to the periphery of action and recognized primarily through the narrative voice and the shaping presence of the author. The self-centered world that defines much of the New Journalism of the 1960s and early 1970s—including earlier works by Mailer, Didion, and McGinniss—is superseded by nonfiction writing that erases, or at least minimizes, private preoccupations and personal history and often privileges a journalist perspective characterized by detachment, restraint, even objectivity.

In *The Executioner's Song*, for example, Mailer meticulously reconstructs the life and death of Gary Gilmore, the Utah native who was convicted of murder and executed by a firing squad in the 1970s. Mailer refrains from direct authorial commentary and presents his material by reconstructing events and describing scenes in great detail. Similarly, in *Cruel Doubt*, McGinniss assumes the role of the detached and seemingly objective narrator and reconstructs the tragic story of the bereaved widow Bonnie Von Stein. Her wealthy and alcoholic husband was viciously murdered in bed while she herself was bludgeoned and stabbed and apparently left for dead. While she fully recovers from her physical injuries, she later discovers that her college-age son, who is more interested in Dungeons and Dragons than textbooks, arranged to have her and Leith Von Stein murdered. While *Cruel Doubt* is a well-written book, and it identifies once again the author's principal thematic interest—father-son relationships—it is not a significant departure from *Fatal Vision* and *Blind Faith*, whereas *The Executioner's Song* is clearly a remarkable and very different achievement for Mailer.

Mailer uncharacteristically removes himself from the center of action and focuses on the life of Gary Gilmore. The self-dramatizing persona and highly conscious literary voice(s) of *The Armies of the Night* are replaced by a narrator who seems to abdicate authorial responsibility by presenting events and information of the Gilmore case as raw, unedited experience. Though Mailer avoids even indirect references to himself, his presence is in part revealed through his interest in Gary Gilmore as the reincarnation of the "white hipster," the existential model of self that was first articulated in "The White Negro" (1958) and later appeared in the characterization of Stephen Rojack, "the reporter," and other figures in both Mailer's fictional and nonfictional writing. Mailer reconstructs the Gilmore story in a flat, prosaic style that reveals the specific language and idioms of a large cast of characters. Their thoughts, comments, and actions, often compressed in brief paragraphs surrounded by an abundance of space, comprise a mosaic-like work that nominally decenters narrative authority by introducing a variety of voices. The book itself is divided into two sections—"Western Voices" and "Eastern Voices"—in which the principal characters are either family and relatives or lawyers and media figures. While the principal story centers on the murders, the trial, and the eventual execution of Gilmore, the book's subtext is an in-depth account of the behind-the-scene hustling that went into securing the rights of the Gilmore story.

Mailer's peculiar authorial silence was not an arbitrary rhetorical choice. In an interview with William Buckley, Mailer explains how writing the book had been a humbling experience. After years of believing he could "dominate any question pretty quickly," he acknowledged that the Gilmore material raised a number of questions for which he could not provide answers. Mailer explains that the "time had come—at least for me in my own work—to do a book where I don't explain it to the reader, and in part I can't explain all of it to the reader."[11] As Mailer's comments suggest, his authorial silence reveals an epistemological relation to the world that identifies a change in his understanding of himself. One of the "remarkable, though somewhat unnerving, achievements of *The Executioner's Song*," Barbara Lounsberry explains, "is that while Mailer has employed metaphor as a means of knowledge (and action) in all his previous nonfiction, in" this work "he uses it to suggest 'not knowing' or the failure to know."[12]

In *Miami*, Joan Didion uses images and language—words like "empty" and "void"—that reveal a similar inability to come to terms with a world that is ultimately unknowable. In fact, Didion reconstructs a metaphorical world, as Mailer does in *The Executioner's Song*, that defies rational understanding. In the opening pages of the book she describes the 2506 Brigade's twenty-fifth anniversary commemoration of the aborted Cuban invasion in 1961. According to Didion, the Bay of Pigs incident "continued to offer Miami an ideal narrative, one in which the men of the 2506 were forever the seducer and betrayer."[13] Throughout *Miami*, Didion periodically points out the various promises (or suggested promises) made to

Cubans about returning to a free Cuba, promises later ignored or forgotten. Didion emphasizes, in fact, that it was not unusual for the CIA to be sponsoring, or at least encouraging, covert action—training men and providing arms—while politicians in Washington were discouraging such action. It is clear, too, that a free Cuba was only an issue, one that might or might not serve the needs of a particular administration. Since John Kennedy's years in office, no American president—not even Ronald Reagan with his persuasive anti-Communist rhetoric—would really provide the military force to overthrow Castro. Still, Miami Cubans believe fervently in *la lucha*—the struggle—which will eventually lead to the overthrow of Castro and the establishment of a free Cuba.

While the Bay of Pigs invasion may provide an ideal story for Miami, Didion maintains that the reality of the Cuban experience might best be seen as an "underwater narrative," a narrative composed of fragments of information, stories of unknown provenance that are impossible to corroborate, many of them involving anti-Castro terrorist groups that momentarily surface and then disappear. Nothing about Miami, according to Didion, was "fixed" or "hard"; "surfaces" tended to merge or disappear, and the day or moment could easily turn into a waking dream or nightmare. For Didion, Christo's huge artwork, *Surrounded Islands*—the ever-changing pink polypropylene fabric surrounding eleven islands—is the metaphorical image that best embodies her idea of Miami.

In all her works of nonfiction, Didion has been preoccupied with telling "stories," stories that are either symbolic, mythical, historical, or personal in nature. In *The White Album*, however, she first began to doubt the validity of all the stories she had told herself and questioned the intelligibility of narrative discourse. This epistemological and personal crisis continued to be, in both *Miami* and *Salvador*, a central point in her work: how to make sense of contemporary experience when codified forms and traditions no longer seem to apply. Didion's reservations, however, reveal as much about her choice of subject matter—and herself—as they do about the ostensibly weak interpretive power of narrative writing. Since the publication of *Slouching Towards Bethlehem*, she has continued to write about social and metaphorical worlds—Haight Ashbury, Salvador, and Miami—in which cultural traditions, history, and basic values and beliefs no longer have the meaning they once did. While the "underwater narrative" of Miami—characterized by terrorism, political dissimulation, racial bigotry, and a cultural and personal myopia shared by seemingly all Miamians—may be rooted in the actual or real, as are the numbers of unexplained killings she discusses in *Salvador*, both worlds are metaphors for, and projections of, Didion's vision (version) of the world.

While the choice of subject matter in the later works of Mailer, Didion, and McGinniss influenced the degree to which they could (or could not) cast themselves as main characters and participate in the experiences they later wrote about, the fact that certain events had transpired does not necessarily preclude more direct authorial involvement, as C.D.B. Bryan's *Friendly Fire* illustrates. It is still possible, for example, for nonfiction writers to define themselves as journalistic detectives, as Woodward and Bernstein do in *All the President's Men*, whose epistemological and principal role is uncovering relevant information and searching for a social or human truth in the aftermath of ostensibly significant social experiences and events. It seems to be significant, nonetheless, that these writers selected material that made personal involvement more difficult or problematic and all but prevented them from focusing on the self as the principal subject of their work. Instead of constructing a journalistic text that focuses on the participatory self as the locus of cultural understanding, and often implicitly defining a self-centered, at times narcissistic, world associated with the ideological perspective of youth (or adolescence), they present a journalistic and personal point of view guided by an adult rationality and the restriction of emotions and passions. In other words, while the ever-watchful ego of a Mailer or a Didion is still at work in these re-imagined worlds, the world is no longer a mirror that validates the primacy of the personal self while it minimizes the capacity for a social construction of identity through the blurring of subject and object, or journalist and world. In fact, decentering the self might be interpreted as an ontological (as well as an epistemological) gesture, revealing the literary journalist's changing relation to the world and identifying an adult (more mature) self that tacitly acknowledges personal finitude and existence of the world outside the specific journalistic contract and occasion. According to Barbara Lounsberry, Mailer's epistemological crisis in *The Executioner's Song* acknowledges this ontological and even transcendent response to secular experience. She explains that Mailer's metaphor of " 'not knowing' or the failure to know . . . suggests the end of the line for Mailer's 'ages of man'—the stage beyond death and re-birth, that of the ultimate unknown."[14]

While Mailer's, Didion's, and McGinniss' distinctive world views and core identities—their values, beliefs, and attitudes—may remain stable from one work to another, even over three or four decades, the manner in which they articulate a journalistic self changes over time and seems to reveal and reflect changes in their lives (growing older) that correspond to socially acceptable ways to talk about and understand the self. As Karl J. Weintraub explains in "Autobiography and Historical Consciousness," "cultures compress the essential values and convictions in human models" that exercise a powerful influence because we assign them a "universal validity" even though they are socially constructed and provisional.[15] McPhee's conceptualization of his characters as ideal citizens, for example, is particularly persuasive because he at once invokes and affirms a conception of self rooted in our past and central to our historical and literary mythology. McPhee conflates a personal understanding of the contemporary self with a historically acceptable—and seemingly transcendent—concept of identity formation.

As I noted throughout this chapter, the most recent works by Mailer, Didion, McGinniss, Thompson, as well as the writings of numerous other literary journalists, tend to minimize personal theatrics and present more modest journalistic and authorial selves. While this change may indeed correspond to patterns and forms of behavior that became more acceptable throughout the 1970s and into the 1980s, it is important to emphasize that individual writers also identify a metaphor of self that reveals their ontological understanding of identity in relation to the worlds—social, political, literary, journalistic—they inhabit and about which they write. The collected writings of this select group of writers reveal variations of the self based on concepts of permanence and change. If McPhee and McGinniss identify an autonomous and timeless (transcendent) model of self informed by idiosyncratic static beliefs about human nature—as essentially good or bad—Didion, Mailer, and Thompson construct a contingent or provisional model of self determined in part by social influences and based on language for its articulation and understanding. To put it in slightly different terms, the works of these and other nonfiction writers illustrate how autobiographical writing might be interpreted, to use Paul John Eakin's words, as a language "always fatally derivative" or as a kind of "original speech, a self-validating testimony to the uniqueness of the self."[16] I would add, as well, that the "self-validating testimony" of the singular or unique self is often a response to social pressures that threaten to obviate personal goals and imperatives; it is as much a form of personal defense—this is evident in the works of Mailer and Thompson—as it is a claim of self-determinacy and individual power. As these comments suggest, the manner in which the self is personally and socially defined and presented is never fixed or stable. The works of Mailer, McGinniss, Wolfe, Didion, Thompson, and McPhee identify one of the recurrent challenges of our literary and cultural experience: to explore thoroughly the complex, ever-changing relationship between the singular self and its world. More specifically, recent works of nonfiction by Mailer, Didion, and others may not constitute, in Michael Schudson's words, "an ideology of the distrust of the self,"[17] but they do raise implicit questions about the sovereignty of the American imperial self within a society that allegedly celebrates the lives of individuals and the social ideology of individualism as well.

Notes

CHAPTER ONE

1. Alfred Kazin, "The Self as History: Reflections on Autobiography," *The American Autobiography: A Collection of Critical Essays*, Albert E. Stone, ed. (Englewood Cliffs, N.J.: Prentice-Hall, 1981), p. 32.

2. Georges Gusdorf, "Conditions and Limits of Autobiography," *Autobiography: Essays Theoretical and Critical*, James Olney, ed. (Princeton, N.J.: Princeton University Press, 1980), p. 29.

3. A. Robert Lee, ed., *First Person Singular: Studies in American Autobiography* (New York: St. Martin's Press, 1988), p. 10.

4. James M. Cox, "Autobiography and America," *Virginia Quarterly Review* 47 (Spring 1971): 262–263.

5. Francis Russell Hart, "History Talking to Itself: Public Personality in Recent Memoir," *New Literary History* 11 (Autumn 1979): 195.

6. Chris Anderson, *Style as Argument: Contemporary American Nonfiction* (Carbondale: Southern Illinois University Press, 1987), p. 2.

7. John J. Pauly, "The Politics of New Journalism," *Literary Journalism in the Twentieth Century*, Norman Sims, ed. (Oxford: Oxford University Press, 1990), p. 112.

8. Anderson, *Style as Argument*, p. 1.

9. Albert E. Stone, *Autobiographical Occasions and Original Acts: Versions of American Identity from Henry Adams to Nate Shaw* (Philadelphia: University of Pennsylvania Press, 1982), p. 13.

10. Michael Schudson, *Discovering the News: A Social History of American Newspapers* (New York: Basic Books, 1978), p. 71.

11. Christopher Lasch, *The Culture of Narcissism: American Life in an Age of Diminishing Expectations* (New York: Warner Books, 1979), p. 165.

12. Geoffrey Galt Harpham, "Conversion and the Language of Autobiography," *Studies in Autobiography*, James Olney, ed. (Oxford: Oxford University Press, 1988), p. 42.

13. Irving Louis Horowitz, "Autobiography as the Presentation of Self for Social Immortality," *New Literary History* 9 (Autumn 1977): 173, 175.

14. Stone, *Autobiographical Occasions and Original Acts*, pp. 14–15.

15. Barbara Lounsberry, "Personal Mythos and the New Journalism: Gay Talese's Fathers and Sons," *Georgia Review* 37 (Fall 1983): 518.

16. James Olney, *Metaphors of Self: The Meaning of Autobiography* (Princeton, N.J.: Princeton University Press, 1972), p. 8.

17. Ibid., p. 32.

18. Ibid.

19. Lee, *First Person Singular*, p. 9.

20. Stone, *The American Autobiography*, p. 3.

CHAPTER TWO

1. Stephen Singular, "Talk with John McPhee," *New York Times Book Review* (28 Nov. 1977): 1.

2. William L. Howarth, ed., "Introduction," *The John McPhee Reader* (New York: Vintage Books, 1977), p. xii.

3. McPhee is not the first journalist from *The New Yorker* to have such freedom; it began when Harold Ross was editor. James Thurber points out "that Ross's major quality as an editor" was his "willingness to give writers a free rein." See Dale Kramer, *Ross and The New Yorker* (New York: Doubleday and Co., 1951), p. 215.

4. Howarth, "Introduction," p. xv.

5. Barbara Lounsberry, *The Art of Fact: Contemporary Artists of Nonfiction* (Westport, Conn.: Greenwood Press, 1990), p. 106.

6. See Kramer, *Ross and The New Yorker*, pp. 118–119. According to Kramer, four elements contributed to a distinct *The New Yorker* style: clarity, casualness, "getting the facts straight," and "a mildly ironical, but paternal attitude toward" New York City.

7. Howarth, "Introduction," p. xiii.

8. Norman Sims, ed., "The Literary Journalists," *The Literary Journalists* (New York: Ballantine Books, 1984), p. 24.

9. John McPhee, "North of the C.P. Line," *Table of Contents* (New York: Farrar, Straus and Giroux, 1985), p. 249.

10. James Olney, "Experience, Metaphor and Meaning: 'The Death of Ivan Illych,' " *Journal of Aesthetics and Art Criticism* 31 (1972): 106.

11. Lounsberry, *The Art of Fact*, pp. 65–106.

12. Irving Louis Horowitz, "Autobiography as the Presentation of Self for Social Immortality," *New Literary History* 9 (Autumn 1977): 173.

13. John McPhee, *Rising from the Plains* (New York: Farrar, Straus and Giroux, 1986), p. 124.

14. John McPhee, *The Headmaster: Frank L. Boyden, of Deerfield* (New York: Farrar, Straus and Giroux, 1966), p. 7.

15. Lounsberry, *The Art of Fact*, p. 89.

16. John McPhee, *Encounters with the Archdruid* (New York: Farrar, Straus and Giroux, 1971), p. 167.

17. John McPhee, "A Forager," *A Roomful of Hovings and Other Profiles* (New York: Farrar, Straus and Giroux, 1968), p. 102.

18. Edward Hoagland, "From John McPhee with Love and Craftsmanship," *New York Times Book Review* (22 June 1975): 3.

19. See pages xviii–xxiii of *The John McPhee Reader* for a detailed account of McPhee's writing habits and his commitment to craftsmanship.

20. John McPhee, *The Survival of the Bark Canoe* (New York: Farrar, Straus and Giroux, 1975), p. 5.

21. McPhee, *Rising from the Plains*, p. 148.

22. McPhee, *The Survival of the Bark Canoe*, pp. 17–18.

23. John McPhee, "Brigade de Cuisine," *Giving Good Weight* (New York: Farrar, Straus and Giroux, 1979), p. 190.

24. McPhee, "A Forager," p. 102.

25. Ibid., p. 75.

26. John McPhee, *A Sense of Where You Are* (New York: Farrar, Straus and Giroux, 1965), p. 28.

27. Kathy Smith, "John McPhee Balances the Act," *Literary Journalism in the Twentieth Century*, Norman Sims, ed. (Oxford: Oxford University Press, 1990), p. 213.

28. McPhee, *A Sense of Where You Are*, p. 21.

29. Ibid., p. 22.

30. John McPhee, *The Pine Barrens* (New York: Farrar, Straus and Giroux, 1968), p. 19.

31. John McPhee, *The Crofter & the Laird* (New York: Farrar, Straus and Giroux, 1970), p. 21.

32. Hoagland, "From John McPhee with Love and Craftsmanship," p. 3.

33. Dennis Drabelle, "A Conversation with John McPhee," *Sierra* (Oct.-Nov.-Dec. 1978): 63.

34. Smith, "John McPhee Balances the Act," p. 212.

35. McPhee, "A Forager," p. 69.

36. Erving Goffman, *The Presentation of Self in Everyday Life* (New York: Anchor Books, 1959), p. 35.

37. McPhee, *The Pine Barrens*, p. 3.

38. Ibid., p. 5.

39. Ibid., p. 4.

40. Ibid., pp. 132–133.

41. John J. Pauly, "The Politics of The New Journalism," *Literary Journalism in the Twentieth Century*, p. 125.

42. Gaye Tuchman, *Making News: A Study in the Construction of Reality* (New York: The Free Press, 1978), p. 89.

43. Michael Schudson, *Discovering the News: A Social History of American Newspapers* (New York: Basic Books, 1978), p. 5.

44. McPhee, *Encounters with the Archdruid*, p. 86.

45. Ibid.

46. John McPhee, "Travels in Georgia," *Pieces of the Frame* (New York: Farrar, Straus and Giroux, 1975), p. 34.

47. Schudson, *Discovering the News*, p. 6.

48. John McPhee, "The Keel of Lake Dickey," *Giving Good Weight* (New York: Farrar, Straus and Giroux, 1979), pp. 137–138.

49. John McPhee, *Oranges* (New York: Farrar, Straus and Giroux, 1967), pp. 61–62.

50. McPhee, *The Crofter & the Laird*, p. 120.

51. McPhee, *The Headmaster*, p. 18.

52. George Roundy, "Crafting Fact: The Prose of John McPhee" (Ph.D. diss., University of Iowa, 1984), p. 30.

53. Wayne C. Booth, *The Rhetoric of Fiction*, 2d ed. (Chicago: University of Chicago Press, 1983), p. 155.

54. Smith, "John McPhee Balances the Act," p. 210.

55. Terry Eagleton, *Literary Theory: An Introduction* (Minneapolis: University of Minnesota Press, 1983), pp. 135–136.

56. Smith, *Literary Journalism in the Twentieth Century*, p. 218.

CHAPTER THREE

1. The biographical information in the first two pages is from the following sources: Charles Moritz, ed., *Current Biography Yearbook 1984* (New York: H. W. Wilson Co., 1984), pp. 268–271; Hal May and James G. Lesniak, eds., *Contemporary Authors* (Detroit: Gale Research, 1989), pp. 268–272.

2. Joe McGinniss, *The Selling of the President 1968* (New York: Pocket Books, 1970), p. 21.

3. Moritz, *Current Biography Yearbook 1984*, p. 270.

4. McGinniss, *The Selling of the President 1968*, p. 23.

5. Ibid., p. 22.

6. Barbara Lounsberry, *The Art of Fact: Contemporary Artists of Nonfiction* (Westport, Conn.: Greenwood Press, 1990), p. 3.

7. Ibid., p. 15.

8. Ibid., p. 3.

9. Joe McGinniss, *Heroes* (New York: Viking Press, 1976), p. 55.

10. Ibid., pp. 65–66.

11. Ibid., pp. 118–119.

12. Ronald Weber, *The Literature of Fact: Literary Nonfiction in American Writing* (Athens: Ohio University Press, 1980), p. 147.

13. McGinniss, *Heroes*, p. 41.

14. Ibid., p. 44.

15. Ibid., p. 43.

16. Ibid.

17. Ibid., p. 23.

18. Ibid., p. 24.

19. Weber, *The Literature of Fact*, p. 147.

20. McGinniss, *Heroes*, p. 176.

21. Joe McGinniss, *Going to Extremes* (New York: Signet Books, 1982), p. 10.

22. Ibid., p. 11.

23. Linda Steiner, "Joe McGinniss," *A Sourcebook of American Literary Journalism: Representative Writers in an Emerging Genre*, Thomas B. Connery, ed. (Westport, Conn.: Greenwood Press, 1992), p. 367.

24. McGinniss, *Going to Extremes*, p. 64.

25. Ibid., p. 83.

26. Ibid., p. 84.

27. Ibid., p. 80.
28. Ibid.
29. Steiner, "Joe McGinniss," *A Sourcebook of American Literary Journalism*, p. 369.
30. Ibid., pp. 370–371.
31. Janet Malcolm, *The Journalist and the Murderer* (New York: Alfred A. Knopf, 1990), p. 17.
32. Ibid., p. 149.
33. Ibid., p. 89.
34. Ibid., p. 141.
35. Ibid., p. 20.
36. Ibid., p. 72.
37. Ibid., p. 144.
38. Joe McGinniss, *Blind Faith* (New York: G. P. Putnam's Sons, 1989), p. 79.
39. Ibid., p. 54.
40. Joe McGinniss, *Fatal Vision* (New York: New American Library, 1983), p. 75.
41. Ibid., p. 76.
42. McGinniss, *Blind Faith*, p. 376.

CHAPTER FOUR

1. Elaine Dundy, "Tom Wolfe . . . But Exactly, Yes,!" *Conversations with Tom Wolfe*, Dorothy Scura, ed. (Jackson: University Press of Mississippi, 1990), p. 15.
2. Toby Thompson, "The Evolution of Dandy Tom," *Conversations with Tom Wolfe*, p. 199.
3. Dundy, "Tom Wolfe . . . But Exactly, Yes,!" p. 15.
4. Thompson, "The Evolution of Dandy Tom," p. 201.
5. Dundy, "Tom Wolfe . . . But Exactly, Yes,!" p. 16.
6. Thompson, "The Evolution of Dandy Tom," p. 206.
7. Terry Coleman, "How to Wolfe a Tangerine at a Tangent," *Conversations with Tom Wolfe*, p. 3.
8. Joe David Bellamy, *The New Fiction: Interviews with Innovative American Writers* (Urbana: University of Illinois Press, 1974), p. 84.
9. Tony Schwartz, "Tom Wolfe: The Great Gadfly," *New York Times Magazine* (20 December 1981): 46.
10. See Chris Anderson, *Style as Argument: Contemporary American Nonfiction* (Carbondale: Southern Illinois University Press, 1987), pp. 8–47.
11. Schwartz, "Tom Wolfe: The Great Gadfly," p. 48.
12. Thompson, "The Evolution of Tom Dandy," p. 206.
13. Ibid.
14. Tom Wolfe, *Mauve Gloves & Madmen, Clutter & Vine* (New York: Bantam Books, 1977), p. 177.
15. Schwartz, "Tom Wolfe: The Great Gadfly," p. 48.
16. Ibid.
17. Ibid.
18. Tom Wolfe, *The Electric Kool-Aid Acid Test* (New York: Bantam Books, 1969), p. 3.
19. Ibid.

20. Chet Flippo, "The Rolling Stone Interview: Tom Wolfe," *Conversations with Tom Wolfe*, p. 149.
21. Philip Nobile, "Wolfe Foresees a Religious 'Great Awakening,' " *Conversations with Tom Wolfe*, p. 95.
22. Tom Wolfe, *Radical Chic & Mau-Mauing the Flak Catchers* (New York: Bantam Books, 1971), p. 118.
23. Ibid., p. 124.
24. Ibid., p. 119.
25. Ibid., pp. 145–146.
26. Tom Wolfe, *The Right Stuff* (New York: Farrar, Straus and Giroux, 1979), p. 25.
27. Ibid., p. 122.
28. Ibid., p. 214.
29. Ibid., p. 269.
30. Ibid., p. 350.
31. Ibid., p. 234.
32. Wolfe, *Radical Chic & Mau-Mauing the Flak Catchers*, p. 25.
33. Wolfe, *The Right Stuff*, pp. 121–122.
34. David Eason, "The New Journalism and the Image-World: Two Modes of Organizing Experience," *Critical Studies in Mass Communications* 1 (Winter 1984): 54.
35. John Hollowell, *Fact & Fiction: The New Journalism and the Nonfiction Novel* (Chapel Hill: University of North Carolina Press, 1977), p. 140.
36. Tom Wolfe, *The Pump House Gang* (New York: Bantam Books, 1969), p. 15.
37. Eason, "The New Journalism and the Image-World: Two Modes of Organizing Experience," p. 52.
38. Wolfe, *The Electric Kool-Aid Acid Test*, p. 47.
39. Elizabeth W. Bruss, "The Game of Literature and Some Literary Games," *New Literary History* 9 (Autumn 1977): 154.
40. Tom Wolfe, *The Painted Word* (New York: Bantam Books, 1975), pp. 14–15.
41. Tom Wolfe, *From Bauhaus to Our House* (New York: Farrar, Straus and Giroux, 1981), p. 18.
42. Wolfe, *Radical Chic & Mau-Mauing the Flak Catchers*, p. 13.
43. Ibid., p. 25.
44. Richard Al Kallan, "Tom Wolfe," *A Sourcebook of American Literary Journalism: Representative Writers in an Emerging Genre*, Thomas B. Connery, ed. (Westport, Conn.: Greenwood Press, 1992), pp. 253–254.
45. Wolfe, *Radical Chic & Mau-Mauing the Flak Catchers*, pp. 53–54.
46. Morris Dickstein, *Gates of Eden: American Culture in the Sixties* (New York: Basic Books, 1977), p. 141.
47. Wolfe, *The Right Stuff*, p. 357.
48. Wolfe, *Radical Chic & Mau-Mauing the Flak Catchers*, p. 129.
49. Christopoher Hitchens, "A Wolfe *in* Chic Clothing," *Mother Jones* (12 January 1983): 18.
50. Ibid., p. 14.
51. Wolfe, *Radical Chic & Mau-Mauing the Flak Catchers*, p. 71.
52. Wolfe, *The Electric Kool-Aid Acid Test*, p. 8.
53. Wolfe, *The Kandy-Kolored Tangerine-Flake Streamline Baby* (New York: Noonday Press, 1965), p. 146.

54. Wolfe, *The Electric Kool-Aid Acid Test*, p. 157.

CHAPTER FIVE

1. Katherine Usher Henderson, *Joan Didion* (New York: Fredrick Ungar Publishing, 1981), p. 3.

2. Ibid., p. 5.

3. Michiko Kakutani, "Joan Didion: Staking Out California," *Joan Didion: Essays and Conversations*, Ellen G. Friedman, ed. (Princeton, N.J.: Ontario Review Press, 1984), p. 35.

4. Sara Davidson, "Joan Didion," *Real Property* (New York: Pocket Books, 1981), p. 83.

5. Henderson, *Joan Didion*, p. 3.

6. Chris Anderson, *Style as Argument: Contemporary American Nonfiction* (Carbondale: Southern Illinois University Press, 1987), p. 172.

7. Gordon O. Taylor, *Chapters of Experience: Studies in Modern American Autobiography* (New York: St. Martin's Press, 1983), p. 139.

8. Alfred Kazin, "The Self as History: Reflections on Autobiography," *The American Autobiography: A Collection of Critical Essays*, Albert E. Stone, ed. (Englewood Cliffs, N.J.: Prentice-Hall, 1981), p. 32.

9. Joan Didion, "Notes from a Native Daughter," *Slouching Towards Bethlehem* (New York: Simon and Schuster, 1968), p. 176.

10. Didion, "On Keeping a Notebook," *Slouching Towards Bethlehem*, p. 139.

11. Patricia Meyer Spacks, "Selves in Hiding," *Women's Autobiography: Essays in Criticism*, Estelle C. Jelinek, ed. (Bloomington: University of Indiana Press, 1980), p. 113.

12. James Olney, *Metaphors of Self: The Meaning of Autobiography* (Princeton, N.J.: Princeton University Press, 1972), p. 14.

13. Didion, "On Keeping a Notebook," p. 133.

14. Ibid., pp. 133–134.

15. Timothy Dow Adams, *Telling Lies in Modern American Autobiography* (Chapel Hill: University of North Carolina Press, 1990), p. 9.

16. Georges Gusdorf, "Conditions and Limits of Autobiography," *Autobiography: Essays Theoretical and Critical*, James Olney, ed. (Princeton, N.J.: Princeton University Press, 1980), p. 38.

17. Didion, "On Keeping a Notebook," p. 136.

18. Ibid.

19. Ibid., 139.

20. Joan Didion, "On Going Home," *Slouching Towards Bethlehem* (New York: Simon and Schuster, 1968), p. 166.

21. Ibid., pp. 167–168.

22. Joan Didion, "Notes from a Native Daughter," *Slouching Towards Bethlehem* (New York: Simon and Schuster, 1968), p. 186.

23. Ibid.

24. Anderson, *Style as Argument: Contemporary American Nonfiction*, p. 139.

25. Didion, "Notes from a Native Daughter," p. 186.

26. Didion, "On Keeping a Notebook," p. 140.

27. Ibid., pp. 140–141.

28. Susan Stamberg, "Cautionary Tales," *Joan Didion: Essays and Conversations*, p. 27.

29. Joan Didion, "Where the Kissing Never Stops," *Slouching Towards Bethlehem* (New York: Simon and Schuster, 1968), p. 51.

30. Ibid., p. 49.

31. Ibid., p. 59.

32. Barbara Lounsberry, *The Art of Fact: Contemporary Artists of Nonfiction* (Westport, Conn.: Greenwood Press, 1990), p. 123.

33. Joan Didion, "On the Morning After the Sixties," *The White Album* (New York: Simon and Schuster, 1979), p. 206.

34. Ibid., p. 207.

35. Joan Didion, "Slouching Towards Bethlehem," *Slouching Towards Bethlehem* (New York: Simon and Schuster, 1968), p. 84.

36. Henderson, *Joan Didion*, p. 103.

37. Didion, "Slouching Towards Bethlehem," p. 128.

38. Anderson, *Style as Argument: Contemporary American Nonfiction*, p. 134.

39. Stamberg, "Cautionary Tales," p. 27.

40. Ibid., p. 26.

41. Joan Didion, "Preface," *Slouching Towards Bethlehem* (New York: Simon and Schuster, 1968), p. xiv.

42. Ibid.

43. Janet Malcolm, *The Journalist and the Murderer* (New York: Alfred A. Knopf, 1990), p. 3.

44. Ibid., pp. 43–44.

45. Stamberg, "Cautionary Tales," p. 26.

46. Albert E. Stone, *Autobiographical Occasions and Original Acts: Versions of American Identity from Henry Adams to Nate Shaw* (Philadelphia: University of Pennsylvania Press, 1982), p. 197.

47. Joan Didion, "Quiet Days in Malibu," *The White Album* (New York: Simon and Schuster, 1979), p. 216.

48. Ibid.

49. Henderson, *Joan Didion*, p. 128.

50. Joan Didion, "Rock of Ages," *Slouching Towards Bethlehem* (New York: Simon and Schuster, 1968), p. 205.

51. Ibid., p. 208.

52. Joan Didion, "At the Dam," *The White Album* (New York: Simon and Schuster, 1979), p. 201.

53. Christopher Lasch, *The Minimal Self: Psychic Survival in Troubled Times* (New York: W. W. Norton and Co., 1984), p. 19.

54. Didion, "Rock of Ages," p. 208.

55. Joan Didion, "Georgia O'Keeffe," *The White Album* (New York: Simon and Schuster, 1979), p. 127.

56. Joan Didion, "The White Album," *The White Album* (New York: Simon and Schuster, 1979), p. 11.

57. Ibid.

58. Ibid., pp. 12–13.

59. Henderson, *Joan Didion*, p. 119.
60. Didion, "The White Album," p. 13.
61. Ibid., pp. 34–35.
62. Ibid., p. 35.
63. Ibid., pp. 11–12.
64. Ibid., p. 12.
65. Ibid., pp. 14–15.
66. Taylor, *Chapters of Experience*, p. 141.
67. Didion, "The White Album," p. 15.
68. Henderson, *Joan Didion*, p. 120.
69. Ibid., p. 121.
70. Joan Didion, "In Bed," *The White Album* (New York: Simon and Schuster, 1979), p. 169.
71. Ibid.
72. Ibid., p. 172.
73. Didion, "Preface," p. xiii.
74. Ibid.
75. Stone, *Autobiographical Occasions and Original Acts*, p. 196.
76. Edwin M. Schur, *Labeling Women Deviant: Gender, Stigma, and Social Control* (Philadelphia: Temple University Press, 1983), p. 25.
77. Norman Mailer, *The Armies of the Night: History as a Novel, the Novel as History* (New York: New American Library, 1968), p. 151.

CHAPTER SIX

1. Timothy Crouse, *The Boys on the Bus* (New York: Ballantine Books, 1974), p. 334.
2. Ibid.
3. Ibid.
4. Hunter S. Thompson, *The Great Shark Hunt* (New York: Summit Books, 1979), p. 14.
5. Craig Vetter, "Playboy Interview: Hunter Thompson," *Playboy* (November 1974): 75.
6. Thompson, *The Great Shark Hunt*, p. 463.
7. Erving Goffman, *Stigma: Notes on the Management of Spoiled Identity* (Englewood Cliffs, N.J.: Prentice-Hall, 1963), p. 9.
8. Hunter S. Thompson, *The Curse of Lono* (New York: Bantam Books, 1983), p. 10.
9. Hunter S. Thompson, *Fear and Loathing: On the Campaign Trail '72* (New York: Popular Library, 1973), p. 24.
10. Ibid., p. 27.
11. Hunter S. Thompson, *Fear and Loathing in Las Vegas: A Savage Journey to the Heart of the American Dream* (New York: Popular Library, 1973), pp. 109–110.
12. Ibid., p. 38.
13. Ibid., p. 56.
14. Erik Erikson, *Life History and the Historical Moment* (New York: W. W. Norton, 1975), p. 20.

15. Thompson, *Fear and Loathing: On the Campaign Trail '72*, p. 248.

16. Wayne C. Booth, "Loathing and Ignorance on the Campaign Trail: 1972," *Columbia Journalism Review* (November 1973): 10.

17. Georges Gusdorf, "Conditions and Limits of Autobiography," *Autobiography: Essays Theoretical and Critical*, James Olney, ed. (Princeton, N.J.: Princeton University Press, 1980), p. 43.

18. John Hellmann, *Fables of Fact: The New Journalism as New Fiction* (Urbana: University of Illinois Press, 1981), p. 69.

19. Jerome Klinkowitz, *The Life of Fiction* (Urbana: University of Illinois Press, 1977), pp. 39–40.

20. Hellmann, *Fables of Fact*, p. 71.

21. Thompson, *Fear and Loathing in Las Vegas*, p. 84.

22. Hunter S. Thompson, *Hell's Angels: A Strange and Terrible Saga* (New York: Ballantine Books, 1967), p. 66.

23. Thompson, *The Great Shark Hunt*, p. 38.

24. Richard Poirier, *The Performing Self: Compositions and Decompositions in the Language of Contemporary Life* (New York: Oxford University Press, 1971), p. 13.

25. Barbara Lounsberry, "Hunter S. Thompson: Redefining the Beast," *Four Quarters* 30 (Summer 1982): 16–23.

26. Thompson, *Hell's Angels*, p. 345.

27. Robert Sam Anson, "The Rolling Stone Sage: Part Two," *New Times* (10 December 1976): 24.

28. Irving Louis Horowitz, "Autobiography as the Presentation of Self for Social Immortality," *New Literary History* 9 (Autumn 1977): 173.

29. Thompson, *Fear and Loathing: On the Campaign Trail '72*, p. 42.

30. Ibid., p. 60.

31. Hellmann, *Fables of Fact*, p. 70.

32. Erving Goffman, *The Presentation of Self in Everyday Life* (Garden City, N.Y.: Anchor Books, 1959), p. 56.

33. Thompson, *The Great Shark Hunt*, p. 33.

34. Thompson, *Fear and Loathing in Las Vegas*, p. 161.

35. Thompson, *Fear and Loathing: On the Campaign Trail '72*, p. 187.

36. Ibid., p. 221.

37. Hellmann, *Fables of Fact*, p. 87.

38. Poirier, *The Performing Self*, p. 43.

CHAPTER SEVEN

1. Norman Mailer, *Advertisements for Myself* (New York: G. P. Putnam's Sons, 1966), p. 85.

2. Ibid., p. 15.

3. John Hollowell, *Fact & Fiction: The New Journalism and the Nonfiction Novel* (Chapel Hill: University of North Carolina Press, 1977), p. 104.

4. Christopher Lasch, *The Culture of Narcissism: American Life in an Age of Diminishing Expectations* (New York: Warner Books, 1979), p. 166.

5. Richard Poirier, *The Performing Self: Compositions and Decompositions in the Languages of Contemporary Life* (New York: Oxford University Press, 1971), p. 14.

6. Norman Mailer, *The Armies of the Night: History as a Novel, the Novel as History* (New York: New American Library, 1968), p. 13.

7. Ibid., p. 14.

8. Hollowell, *Fact & Fiction*, p. 92.

9. Mailer, *The Armies of the Night*, p. 16.

10. Malini Johar Schueller, *The Politics of Voice: Liberalism and Social Criticism from Franklin to Kingston* (Albany: State University of New York Press, 1992), p. 125.

11. Poirier, *The Performing Self*, p. 14.

12. Chris Anderson, *Style as Argument: Contemporary American Nonfiction* (Carbondale: Southern Illinois University Press, 1987), p. 96.

13. Ibid., p. 97.

14. Mailer, *The Armies of the Night*, p. 30.

15. Ibid., p. 106.

16. Ibid., p. 153.

17. Ibid., p. 33.

18. Barbara Lounsberry, *The Art of Fact: Contemporary Artists of Nonfiction* (Westport, Conn.: Greenwood Press, 1990), p. 140.

19. Mailer, *The Armies of the Night*, p. 128.

20. Ibid., p. 129.

21. Ibid., p. 73.

22. Ibid., p. 93.

23. Ibid., p. 163.

24. Ibid., p. 166.

25. Ibid., p. 153.

26. Schueller, *The Politics of Voice*, p. 133.

27. Barry Leeds, *The Structured Vision of Norman Mailer* (New York: New York University Press, 1969), p. 250.

28. Mailer, *The Armies of the Night*, p. 20.

29. Andrew Gordon, *An American Dreamer: A Psychoanalytic Study of the Fiction of Norman Mailer* (Madison, N.J.: Fairleigh Dickinson University Press, 1980), pp. 189–192.

30. Norman Mailer, *Miami and the Siege of Chicago: An Informal History of the Republican and Democratic Conventions of 1968*. (New York: New American Library, 1968), p. 220.

31. Ibid., pp. 220–221.

32. Mailer, *The Armies of the Night*, p. 39.

33. Ibid., p. 58.

34. Poirier, *The Performing Self*, p. 105.

35. Hollowell, *Fact & Fiction*, p. 97.

36. Ibid., p. 97.

37. Mailer, *The Armies of the Night*, p. 149.

38. Ibid., p. 123.

39. Ibid., p. 126.

40. Mailer, *Miami and the Siege of Chicago*, p. 145.

41. Mailer, *The Armies of the Night*, p. 78.

42. Ibid.

43. Poirier, *The Performing Self*, 104.

44. Mailer, *The Armies of the Night*, p. 59.
45. Ibid., p. 83.
46. Ibid., p. 84.
47. Poirier, *The Performing Self*, p. 105.
48. Mailer, *The Armies of the Night*, p. 216.
49. Ibid., p. 224.
50. Ibid., p. 225.
51. Ibid., pp. 171–172.
52. John Hellmann, *Fables of Fact: The New Journalism as New Fiction* (Urbana: University of Illinois Press, 1981), p. 44.
53. Ibid., p. 42.
54. Francis Russell Hart, "History Talking to Itself: Public Personality in Recent Memoir," *New Literary History* 11 (Autumn 1979): 193.
55. Gordon, *An American Dreamer*, p. 188.
56. Robert Merrill, *Norman Mailer* (Boston: Twayne Publishers, 1978), pp. 120–122.
57. Mailer, *The Armies of the Night*, p. 238.

CHAPTER EIGHT

1. Francis Russell Hart, "History Talking to Itself: Public Personality in Recent Memoir," *New Literary History* 11 (Autumn 1979): 209.
2. Joe McGinniss, *Going to Extremes* (New York: Signet Books, 1982), p. 10.
3. Jonathan Raban, *Old Glory: An American Voyage* (New York: Penguin Books, 1982), p. 16.
4. William Least Heat Moon, *Blue Highways: A Journey into America* (Boston: Little, Brown and Co., 1982), p. 3.
5. Raban, *Old Glory*, p. 16.
6. Ibid., p. 278.
7. Ibid., p. 394.
8. Least Heat Moon, *Blue Highways*, p. 406.
9. Ibid., p. 411.
10. Philip G. Terrie, "River of Paradox: John McPhee's 'The Encircled River,'" *Western American Literature* 23 (May 1988): 5.
11. An interview with Norman Mailer, *Firing Line* (11 October 1979). Quoted from Barbara Lounsberry, *The Art of Fact: Contemporary Artists of Nonfiction* (Westport, Conn.: Greenwood Press, 1990), p. 187.
12. Lounsberry, *The Art of Fact*, p. 181.
13. Joan Didion, *Miami* (New York: Simon and Schuster, 1987), p. 19.
14. Lounsberry, *The Art of Fact*, p. 181.
15. Karl J. Weintraub, "Autobiography and Historical Consciousness," *Critical Inquiry* 1 (June 1975): 837.
16. Paul John Eakin, *Fictions in Autobiography: Studies in the Art of Self-Invention* (Princeton, N.J.: Princeton University Press, 1985), p. 182.
17. Michael Schudson, *Discovering the News: A Social History of Newspapers* (New York: Basic Books, 1978), p. 71.

Bibliography

Adams, Timothy Dow. *Telling Lies in Modern American Autobiography.* Chapel Hill: University of North Carolina Press, 1990.

Anderson, Chris. *Style as Argument: Contemporary American Nonfiction.* Carbondale: Southern Illinois University Press, 1987.

Anson, Robert Sam. "The Rolling Stone Saga: Part Two." *New Times* (10 December 1976): 22–37, 54–61.

Armstrong, David. A *Trumpet to Arms: Alternative Media in America.* Los Angeles: J. P. Tarcher, 1981.

Bellamy, Joe David. *The New Fiction: Interviews with Innovative American Writers.* Urbana: University of Illinois Press, 1974.

Berger, Peter L., and Thomas Luckmann. *The Social Construction of Reality: A Treatise in the Sociology of Knowledge.* New York: Anchor Books, 1967.

Bernstein, Carl, and Robert Woodward. *All the President's Men.* New York: Simon and Schuster, 1974.

Bly, Carol. *Letters from the Country.* New York: Harper and Row, 1981.

Boorstin, Daniel. *The Image: A Guide to Pseudo-Events in America.* New York: Atheneum, 1978.

Booth, Wayne C. "Loathing and Ignorance on the Campaign Trail: 1972." *Columbia Journalism Review* (November 1973): 7–12.

———. *The Rhetoric of Fiction*, 2d ed. Chicago: University of Chicago Press, 1983.

Brown, Richard. *A Poetic for Sociology: Toward a Logic of Discovery for the Human Sciences.* Cambridge: Cambridge University Press, 1977.

Bruss, Elizabeth W. "The Game of Literature and Some Literary Games." *New Literary History* 9 (Autumn 1977): 153–172.

Bryan, C.D.B. *Friendly Fire.* New York: G. P. Putnam's Sons, 1976.

Bugliosi, Vincent. *Helter Skelter.* New York: W. W. Norton and Co., 1974.

Clecak, Peter. *America's Quest for the Ideal Self: Dissent and Fulfillment in the 60s and 70s.* Oxford: Oxford University Press, 1983.

Cohen, Mabel Blake, M.D. "Personal Identity and Sexual Identity." *Psychoanalysis and Women*. Jean Baker Miller, M.D., ed. New York: Penguin Books, 1973.

Connery, Thomas B. *A Sourcebook of American Literary Journalism: Representative Writers in an Emerging Genre*. Westport, Conn.: Greenwood Press, 1992.

Cox, James. "Autobiography and America." *Virginia Quarterly Review* 47 (1971): 251–277.

Crouse, Timothy. *The Boys on the Bus*. New York: Ballantine Books, 1974.

Davidson, Sarah. "Joan Didion." *Real Property*. New York: Pocket Books, 1981.

Dennis, Everette E., and William L. Rivers. *Other Voices: The New Journalism in America*. San Francisco: Canfield Press, 1974.

Dickstein, Morris. *Gates of Eden: American Culture in the Sixties*. New York: Basic Books, 1977.

Didion, Joan. *Slouching Towards Bethlehem*. New York: Simon and Schuster, 1968.

———. *The White Album*. New York: Simon and Schuster, 1979.

———. *Salvador*. New York: Washington Square Press, 1983.

———. *Miami*. New York: Simon and Schuster, 1987.

Drabelle, Dennis. "A Conversation with John McPhee." *Sierra* (Oct.-Nov.-Dec. 1978): 61–63.

Dunne, John Gregory. *Vegas*. New York: Warner Books, 1974.

Eagleton, Terry. *Literary Theory: An Introduction*. Minneapolis: University of Minnesota Press, 1983.

Eakin, Paul John. *Fictions in Autobiography: Studies in the Art of Self-Invention*. Princeton, N.J.: Princeton University Press, 1985.

Eason, David. "Metajournalism: The Problem of Reporting in the Nonfiction Novel." Ph.D. diss., Southern Illinois University at Carbondale, 1977.

———. "The New Journalism and the Image-World: Two Modes of Organizing Experience." *Critical Studies in Mass Communications* 1 (Winter 1984): 51–65.

Ehrenreich, Barbara. *The Hearts of Men: American Dreams and the Flight from Commitment*. New York: Anchor Books, 1984.

Ehrlich, Gretel. *The Solace of Open Spaces*. New York: Viking Penguin Books, 1985.

Ephron, Nora. *Crazy Salad: Some Things about Women*. New York: Pocket Books, 1976.

Erikson, Erik. *Life History and the Historical Moment*. New York: W. W. Norton, 1975.

Goffman, Erving. *The Presentation of Self in Everyday Life*. Garden City, N.Y.: Anchor Books, 1959.

———. *Stigma: Notes on the Management of Spoiled Identity*. Englewood Cliffs, N.J.: Prentice-Hall, 1963.

Gordon, Andrew. *An American Dreamer: A Psychoanalytic Study of the Fiction of Norman Mailer*. Madison, N.J.: Fairleigh Dickinson University Press, 1980.

Gusdorf, Georges. "Conditions and Limits of Autobiography." *Autobiography: Essays Theoretical and Critical*. James Olney, ed. Princeton, N.J.: Princeton University Press, 1980.

Hampl, Patricia. *A Romantic Education*. Boston: Houghton Mifflin, 1981.

Harpham, Geoffrey Galt. "Conversion and the Language of Autobiography." *Studies in Autobiography*. James Olney, ed. Oxford: Oxford University Press, 1988.

Harrison, Barbara Grizzuti. "Joan Didion: The Courage of Her Afflictions." *The Nation* (29 September 1979): 277–286.

Hart, Francis Russell. "History Talking to Itself: Public Personality in Recent Memoir." *New Literary History* 11 (Autumn 1979): 193–210.

Hebdige, Dick. *Subculture: The Meaning of Style*. London: Methuen, 1979.

Hellmann, John. *Fables of Fact: The New Journalism as New Fiction*. Urbana: University of Illinois Press, 1981.

Henderson, Katherine Usher. *Joan Didion*. New York: Fredrick Ungar Publishing, 1981.

Hersh, Seymour. *My Lai 4: A Report on the Massacre and Its Aftermath*. New York: Random House, 1970.

Hitchens, Christopher. "*A* Wolfe *in* Chic Clothing." *Mother Jones* (12 January 1983): 12–18.

Hoagland, Edward. "From John McPhee with Love and Craftsmanship." *New York Times Book Review* (22 June 1975): 3.

Hollowell, John. *Fact & Fiction: The New Journalism and the Nonfiction Novel*. Chapel Hill: University of North Carolina Press, 1977.

Horowitz, Irving Louis. "Autobiography as the Presentation of Self for Social Immortality." *New Literary History* 9 (Autumn 1977): 173–179.

Howarth, William L., ed. *The John McPhee Reader*. New York: Vintage Books, 1977.

Jones, Dan. "The Fiction of Fact: Toward a Journalistic Aesthetic." Ph.D. diss., University of Iowa, 1984.

Kakutani, Michiko. "The Writing in the Rocks." *New York Times Book Review* (1 January 1983): 20.

———. "Joan Didion: Staking Out California." *Joan Didion: Essays and Conversations*. Ellen G. Friedman, ed. Princeton, N.J.: Ontario Review Press, 1984.

Kazin, Alfred. "The Self as History: Reflections on Autobiography." *The American Autobiography: A Collection of Critical Essays*. Albert E. Stone, ed. Englewood Cliffs, N.J.: Prentice-Hall, 1981.

Klinkowitz, Jerome. *The Life of Fiction*. Urbana: University of Illinois Press, 1977.

Kramer, Dale. *Ross and The New Yorker*. New York: Doubleday and Co., 1951.

Kramer, Jane. *The Last Cowboy*. New York: Pocket Books, 1977.

Kramer, Mark. *Three Farms: Making Milk, Meat, and Money from the American Soil*. New York: Bantam Books, 1981.

———. *Invasive Procedures*. New York: Harper and Row, 1983.

Lasch, Christopher. *The Culture of Narcissism: American Life in an Age of Diminishing Expectations*. New York: Warner Books, 1979.

———. *The Minimal Self: Psychic Survival in Troubled Times*. New York: W. W. Norton and Co., 1984.

Least Heat Moon, William. *Blue Highways: A Journey into America*. Boston: Little, Brown and Co., 1982.

Lee, A. Robert, ed. *First Person Singular: Studies in American Autobiography*. New York: St. Martin's Press, 1988.

Leeds, Barry. *The Structured Vision of Norman Mailer*. New York: New York University Press, 1969.

Lounsberry, Barbara. "Hunter S. Thompson: Redefining the Beast." *Four Quarters* 30 (Summer 1982): 16–23.

———. "Personal Mythos and the New Journalism: Gay Talese's Fathers and Sons." *Georgia Review* 37 (Fall 1983): 517–529.

———. *The Art of Fact: Contemporary Artists of Nonfiction*. Westport, Conn.: Greenwood Press, 1990.
MacLean, Maria. *Narrative as Performance: The Baudelairean Experiment*. London and New York: Routledge, 1988.
Mailer, Norman. *Advertisements for Myself*. New York: G. P. Putnam's Sons, 1966.
———. *The Armies of the Night: History as a Novel, The Novel as History*. New York: New American Library, 1968.
———. *Miami and the Siege of Chicago: An Informal History of the Republican and Democratic Conventions of 1968*. New York: New American Library, 1968.
———. *Of a Fire on the Moon*. Boston: Little, Brown and Co., 1970.
———. *The Fight*. Boston: Little, Brown and Co., 1975.
———. *The Executioner's Song*. Boston: Little, Brown and Co., 1979.
Malcolm, Janet. *The Journalist and the Murderer*. New York: Alfred A. Knopf, 1990.
Matthiessen, Peter. *The Snow Leopard*. New York: Bantam Books, 1978.
May, Hal, and James G. Lesniak, eds. *Contemporary Authors*. Detroit: Gale Research, 1989.
McGinniss, Joe. *The Selling of the President 1968*. New York: Pocket Books, 1970.
———. *Heroes*. New York: Viking Press, 1976.
———. *Going to Extremes*. New York: Signet Books, 1982.
———. *Fatal Vision*. New York: New American Library, 1983.
———. *Blind Faith*. New York: G. P. Putnam's Sons, 1989.
———. *Cruel Doubt*. New York: Pocket Star Books, 1992.
McPhee, John. *A Sense of Where You Are*. New York: Farrar, Straus and Giroux, 1965.
———. *The Headmaster: Frank L. Boyden, of Deerfield*. Farrar, Straus and Giroux, 1966.
———. *Oranges*. New York: Farrar, Straus and Giroux, 1967.
———. *The Pine Barrens*. New York: Farrar, Straus and Giroux, 1968.
———. *A Roomful of Hovings and Other Profiles*. New York: Farrar, Straus and Giroux, 1968.
———. *The Crofter & the Laird*. New York: Farrar, Straus and Giroux, 1970.
———. *Encounters with the Archdruid*. New York: Farrar, Straus and Giroux, 1971.
———. *Pieces of the Frame*. New York: Farrar, Straus and Giroux, 1975.
———. *The Survival of the Bark Canoe*. New York: Farrar, Straus and Giroux, 1975.
———. *Coming into the Country*. New York: Farrar, Straus and Giroux, 1976.
———. *Giving Good Weight*. New York: Farrar, Straus and Giroux, 1979.
———. *Basin and Range*. New York: Farrar, Straus and Giroux, 1980.
———. *In Suspect Terrain*. New York: Farrar, Straus and Giroux, 1982.
———. *Table of Contents*. New York: Farrar, Straus and Giroux, 1985.
———. *Rising from the Plains*. New York: Farrar, Straus and Giroux, 1986.
———. *The Control of Nature*. New York: Farrar, Straus and Giroux, 1989.
Merrill, Robert. *Norman Mailer*. Boston: Twayne Publishers, 1978.
Moritz, Charles, ed. *Current Biography Yearbook 1984*. New York: H. W. Wilson Co., 1984.
Olney, James. "Experience, Metaphor, and Meaning: 'The Death of Ivan Illych.' " *Journal of Aesthetics and Art Criticism* 31 (1972): 101–114.
———. *Metaphors of Self: The Meaning of Autobiography*. Princeton, N.J.: Princeton University Press, 1972.

Pirsig, Robert M. *Zen and the Art of Motorcycle Maintenance*. New York: Bantam Books, 1974.

Poirier, Richard. *The Performing Self: Compositions and Decompositions in the Language of Contemporary Life*. New York: Oxford University Press, 1971.

Raban, Jonathan. *Old Glory: An American Voyage*. New York: Penguin Books, 1982.

Renza, Louis A. "The Veto of the Imagination: A Theory of Autobiography." *New Literary History* 9 (1977): 1–26.

Rhodes, Richard. *The Inland Ground: An Evocation of the American Middle West*. New York: Atheneum, 1970.

———. *Looking for America: A Writer's Odyssey*. Garden City, N.Y.: Doubleday, 1979.

———. *The Making of the Atomic Bomb*. New York: Touchstone, 1988.

Riesman, David. *The Lonely Crowd*, abridged edition. New Haven, Conn.: Yale University Press, 1968.

Roundy, George. "Crafting Fact: The Prose of John McPhee." Ph.D. diss., University of Iowa, 1984.

Rubin, Jerry. *Growing (up) at Thirty-Seven*. New York: M. Evans and Co., 1983.

Sayre, Robert. "The Proper Study: Autobiography in American Studies." *The American Autobiography: A Collection of Critical Essays*. Albert E. Stone, ed. Englewood Cliffs, N.J.: Prentice-Hall, 1981.

Schudson, Michael. *Discovering the News: A Social History of American Newspapers*. New York: Basic Books, 1978.

Schueller, Malini Johar. *The Politics of Voice: Liberalism and Social Criticism from Franklin to Kingston*. Albany: State University of New York Press, 1992.

Schur, Edwin M. *Labeling Women Deviant: Gender, Stigma, and Social Control*. Philadelphia: Temple University Press, 1983.

Schwartz, Tony. "Tom Wolfe: The Great Gadfly." *New York Times Magazine* (20 December 1981): 46–62.

Scura, Dorothy, ed. *Conversations with Tom Wolfe*. Jackson: University Press of Mississippi, 1990.

Sheed, Wilfred. "The Good Word: A Fun-House Mirror." *New York Times Book Review* (3 December 1972): 4.

Sims, Norman, ed. *The Literary Journalists*. New York: Ballantine Books, 1984.

———. *Literary Journalism in the Twentieth Century*. Oxford: Oxford University Press, 1990.

Singular, Stephen. "Talk with John McPhee." *New York Times Book Review* (28 Nov. 1977): 1.

Spacks, Patricia Meyer. "Selves in Hiding." *Women's Autobiography: Essays in Criticism*. Estelle C. Jelinek, ed. Bloomington: University of Indiana Press, 1980.

———. "Stages of Self: Notes on Autobiography and the Life Cycle." *The American Autobiography: A Collection of Critical Essays*. Albert E. Stone, ed. Englewood Cliffs, N.J.: Prentice-Hall, 1981.

Sprinker, Michael. "Fictions of the Self: The End of Autobiography." *Autobiography: Essays Theoretical and Critical*. James Olney, ed. Princeton: Princeton University Press, 1980.

Stamberg, Susan. "Cautionary Tales." *Joan Didion: Essays and Conversations*. Ellen G. Friedman, ed. Princeton, N.J.: Ontario Review Press, 1984.

Steinem, Gloria. *Outrageous Acts and Everyday Rebellions*. New York: Signet, 1986.

Stone, Albert E., ed. *The American Autobiography: A Collection of Critical Essays*. Englewood Cliffs, N.J.: Prentice-Hall, 1981.

———. *Autobiographical Occasions and Original Acts: Versions of American Identity from Henry Adams to Nate Shaw*. Philadelphia: University of Pennsylvania Press, 1982.

Stout, Janis. *The Journey Narrative in American Literature: Patterns and Departures*. Westport, Conn.: Greenwood Press, 1983.

Street, John. *Rebel Rock: The Politics of Popular Music*. Oxford: Basil Blackwell, 1986.

Taylor, Gordon O. *Chapters of Experience: Studies in Modern American Autobiography*. New York: St. Martin's Press, 1983.

Terrie, Philip G. "River of Paradox: John McPhee's 'The Encircled River.' " *Western American Literature* 23 (May 1988): 3–15.

Thompson, Hunter S. *Hell's Angels: A Strange and Terrible Saga*. New York: Ballantine Books, 1967.

———. *Fear and Loathing: On the Campaign Trail '72*. New York: Popular Library, 1973.

———. *Fear and Loathing in Las Vegas: A Savage Journey to the Heart of the American Dream*. New York: Popular Library, 1973.

———. *The Great Shark Hunt*. New York: Summit Books, 1979.

———. *The Curse of Lono*. New York: Bantam Books, 1983.

———. *Generation of Swine: Tales of Shame and Degradation in the '80's*. New York: Summit Books, 1988.

Tuchman, Gaye. *Making News: A Study in the Construction of Reality*. London: The Free Press, 1978.

Vetter, Craig. "Playboy Interview: Hunter Thompson." *Playboy* (November 1974), 75–90, 245–246.

Vonnegut, Mark. *The Eden Express*. New York: Praeger, 1975.

Wambaugh, Joseph. *The Onion Field*. New York: Delacorte Press, 1973.

Weber, Ronald, ed. *The Reporter As Artist: A Look at the New Journalism Controversy*. New York: Hasting House, 1974.

———. *The Literature of Fact: Nonfiction in American Writing*. Athens: Ohio University Press, 1980.

Weintraub, Karl J. "Autobiography and Historical Consciousness." *Critical Inquiry* 1 (June 1975): 821–848.

Wilkinson, Alec. *Moonshine: A Life in Pursuit of White Liquor*. New York: Penguin Books, 1985.

Winchell, Mark Royden. *Joan Didion*. Twayne United States Authors Series. Boston: Twayne Publishers, 1980.

Wolfe, Tom. *The Kandy-Kolored Tangerine-Flake Streamline Baby*. New York: Noonday Press, 1965.

———. *The Electric Kool-Aid Acid Test*. New York: Bantam Books, 1969.

———. *The Pump House Gang*. New York: Bantam Books, 1969.

———. *Radical Chic & Mau-Mauing the Flak Catchers*. New York: Bantam Books, 1971.

———. *The Painted Word*. New York: Bantam Books, 1975.

———. *Mauve Gloves & Madmen, Clutter & Vine*. New York: Bantam Books, 1977.

———. *The Right Stuff*. New York: Farrar, Straus and Giroux, 1979.

———. *From Bauhaus to Our House*. New York: Farrar, Straus and Giroux, 1981.

Wolfe, Tom and E. W. Johnson, eds. *The New Journalism*. New York: Harper and Row, 1973.

Zavarzadeh, Mas'ud. *The Mythopoeic Reality: The Postwar American Nonfiction Novel*. Urbana: University of Illinois Press, 1976.

Index

ABOUT THE AUTHOR

JAMES N. STULL is Assistant Adjunct Professor in the Department of English at Iowa State University. His academic specialties include contemporary nonfiction, American literature, and advertising and other aspects of popular culture. His publications in these areas have appeared in the *Connecticut Review*, the *North Dakota Quarterly*, the *Canadian Review of American Studies*, and the *Journal of Popular Culture*.

ISBN 0-313-28825-9
EAN
9 780313 288258 90000>
HARDCOVER BAR CODE